THE SEVEN MYTHS OF
CUSTOMER MANAGEMENT

THE SEVEN MYTHS OF CUSTOMER MANAGEMENT

How to be customer-driven without being customer-led

John Abram
Paul Hawkes

JOHN WILEY & SONS, LTD

Copyright © 2003   John Wiley & Sons Ltd, The Atrium, Southern Gate, Chichester, West Sussex PO19 8SQ, England

Telephone (+44) 1243 779777

Email (for orders and customer service enquiries): cs-books@wiley.co.uk
Visit our Home Page on www.wileyeurope.com or www.wiley.com

This publication is designed to provide accurate and authoritative information in regard to the subject matter covered. It is sold on the understanding that the Publisher is not engaged in rendering professional services. If professional advice or other expert assistance is required, the services of a competent professional should be sought.

Other Wiley Editorial Offices

John Wiley & Sons Inc., 111 River Street, Hoboken, NJ 07030, USA

Jossey-Bass, 989 Market Street, San Francisco, CA 94103-1741, USA

Wiley-VCH Verlag GmbH, Boschstr. 12, D-69469 Weinheim, Germany

John Wiley & Sons Australia Ltd, 33 Park Road, Milton, Queensland 4064, Australia

John Wiley & Sons (Asia) Pte Ltd, 2 Clementi Loop #02-01, Jin Xing Distripark, Singapore 129809

John Wiley & Sons Canada Ltd, 22 Worcester Road, Etobicoke, Ontario, Canada M9W 1L1

Wiley also publishes its books in a variety of electronic formats. Some content that appears in print may not be available in electronic books.

Library of Congress Cataloging-in-Publication Data

Hawkes, Paul.
    The seven myths of customer management: how to be customer-driven without being customer-led / Paul Hawkes, John Abram.
        p. cm.
Includes bibliographical references and index.
    ISBN 0-470-85880-X (cloth : alk. paper)
    1. Customer relations – Management. I. Abram, John. II. Title.
    HF5415.5.H375 2003
    658.8'12 – dc21   2003007516

British Library Cataloguing in Publication Data

A catalogue record for this book is available from the British Library

ISBN 0-470-85880-X

Typeset in 11/14 Palatino by SNP Best-set Typesetter Ltd., Hong Kong
Printed and bound in Great Britain by TJ International Ltd, Padstow, Cornwall
This book is printed on acid-free paper responsibly manufactured from sustainable forestry in which at least two trees are planted for each one used for paper production.

Contents

Figures   ix

Acknowledgements   xi

Introduction   xii

1 The seven myths of customer management:
   Debunking some established wisdom   1

   The dangers of customer leadership   1
   What is really happening?   5
   Myth 1: Customer retention is the key to increased
       profitability   6
   Myth 2: Divesting unprofitable customers will increase
       profitability overall   9
   Myth 3: Customer satisfaction leads to customer loyalty   12
   Myth 4: Repeat purchase is the same as customer loyalty   15
   Myth 5: Organizations should develop relationships
       with their customers   18
   Myth 6: One-to-one marketing is the ultimate goal   21
   Myth 7: Technology is the primary enabler of customer
       focus   25
   A different approach   28

2 Testing the water: Understanding where you are today   29

    Picking up customer signals   32
    Business-to-business customers   36
    What research does not tell you   39
    New technology, new danger   42
    Substituting benchmarking for thought   44
    Ten ways to gain real customer insight   46

3 Look before you leap: Developing a customer-focused
    strategy   50

    What is customer-focused strategy?   52
    Strategy in context   55
    Developing customer-focused strategy   58
    Appraising the world outside   62
    Seeking to be different   66
    Leading on cost   69
    Focusing on markets or customers   70
    The customer lifecycle   73
    Deciding and evaluating alternatives   77
    Action planning   80

4 Measuring your way to success: Allocating resources
    for maximum effect   83

    The failure of measurement   85
    Customer attitude measures   86
    Customer retention measures   87
    Customer value measures   89
    The failure of management information systems   93
    Towards customer value   97
    Customer value analysis in action   102
    The pitfalls and problems   107
    The benefits of value-based management   109

5 Don't keep it too simple, stupid: The need for a
    segmented approach   111

    Segment or die   113
    Understanding customers' needs and motivations   114

Collecting the data   120
From data to intelligence   120
From intelligence to hypothesis   126
From hypothesis to appraisal   130
From appraisal to strategy   131
From strategy to results   133
Pitfalls and problems   136
Segmentation: a postscript   138

6 Lining up the ducks: Aligning the company for
   customer focus   140

   Aligning finance   142
   Aligning product strategy   143
   Aligning the proposition: from product to profit   146
   Brand alignment   148
   Aligning distribution   150
   Aligning customer communication   152
   Loyalty programmes   158
   Alignment: a postscript   163

7 Are you the problem? The role of leadership in
   creating customer focus   164

   Data-less decision making   166
   Rearranging the deckchairs   168
   The pitfalls of project teams   169
   Best practice is sometimes best left alone   170
   Incentivizing inappropriate behaviour   172
   Technology turmoil   175
   Everyone embraces change enthusiastically   179
   Reorganizing for focus   183
   Changing a light bulb   187

8 Bringing the focus alive: A practical action plan   188

   An action plan for customer focus   190
   Managing the customer focus process   190
   The internal review   193

Customer dynamics and needs 195
Segment objectives and propositions 198
Customer-management objectives, strategy and tactics 200
Channel strategies and implementation 207
Testing and performance measurement 208
Customer and market knowledge management 211
Change planning 213
Technology strategy 214

Index 218

Figures

1.1	Travel company customer contribution	8
1.2	The satisfaction/loyalty matrix	14
1.3	Satisfaction vs loyalty: retail bank	15
2.1	Importance vs performance	45
3.1	Strategy formulation	58
3.2	Generic competitive strategies	61
3.3	Competitive forces analysis	62
3.4	The profit hierarchy	65
3.5	The Ansoff matrix	65
3.6	The differentiation matrix	67
3.7	The cost/differentiation matrix	72
3.8	The customer lifecycle	73
3.9	The risk/revenue matrix	78
3.10	Investment vs implementation	78
3.11	Gap analysis and strategy alternatives	79
4.1	Attrition by customer life stage	89
4.2	Reasons for credit-card closure	90
4.3	Customer revenues vs costs	97
4.4	The customer value matrix	100
4.5	The customer value management cube	101
4.6	Calculating customer value	103
4.7	Segmented lifetime values	105

4.8	Value segment analysis	106
5.1	Credit-card market segmentation	116
5.2	Segmentation by buyer behaviour	118
5.3	Segmentation analysis by customer number	119
5.4	Segmentation analysis by customer value	119
5.5	Purchase frequency by customer longevity	122
5.6	Customer age by annual purchase value	123
5.7	Customer value by source	124
5.8	Pareto analysis	125
5.9	The customer value management cube	127
5.10	Segmentation hypothesis	132
5.11	Segmentation by strategic intent	133
6.1	Customer-focused new product development	146
6.2	The customer investment/profit paradox	155
6.3	Consumer loyalty programmes: the strategic rationale	161
7.1	Managing customer-focused change	181
8.1	A customer focus action plan	190
8.2	Forgetting a lousy day . . .	203
8.3	Furniture manufacturer customer-segmentation model	205

Acknowledgements

Although this book has been written by just two people, many hundreds of others have helped us, albeit unwittingly. They are too numerous to mention by name, but they include all our colleagues at Abram, Hawkes *plc* as well as the many clients who were trusting enough to hire us. We had 15 years of learning, stimulation and fun. Our thanks are due to everyone we worked with.

Our thanks also to Valoris Ltd, the company that acquired Abram, Hawkes, for giving us access to many of the illustrations and examples in this book.

Introduction

In 1987 we founded a consultancy that specialized in market and customer management. Our work centred on helping our clients make more money by increasing their revenues. While we also advised on how to reduce costs or change processes, the majority of our activity was directed at improving the efficiency, effectiveness and, critically, the profitability of our clients' operations by growing the value of the customers they served.

Over the course of the following 15 years, we were able to work with some of the UK's largest and most successful companies, across many industries. We observed a wide range of strategies being implemented by an extraordinary array of senior managers, who adopted a diverse set of management styles and techniques to address many and varied business challenges.

Irrespective of the differences in objectives, strategies and styles, there was always one common factor. Every organization with which we worked (without exception) relied on its customers to generate the income that paid the bills, the salaries and, of course, our fees! Notwithstanding the ability of financiers to move a company's share price by fancy manipulation such as off-balance-sheet financing, this same income is the fundamental and, arguably, the only lasting source of long-term shareholder value.

Although we worked in an exceptionally competitive consultancy market and competed against firms that were many times larger than our own, we nevertheless grew our practice steadily, year by year developing a blue-chip client list and a top-quality consulting team. The success of our business undoubtedly stemmed from our focus on generating profit for our clients by maximizing the value of both existing and potential customers. Of course all our competitors had something to say on the subject too, but what we said was, usually, quite different. Fortunately, it was sufficiently compelling that organizations as diverse as Thomas Cook, Norwich Union, GUS and Switch, to name just four, were prepared to listen and take our advice.

The fundamental beliefs that governed our approach can be summarized as follows:

- Customers are an asset of the business and the primary source of long-term shareholder value.
- Like any other asset, customers have to be managed positively to maximize the return on the investment in them.
- Unlike any other asset, customers constantly change and thus a deep and insightful understanding is required to manage them successfully.
- Any investment in the acquisition or ongoing management of customers must only be made if there is an acceptable probability that the investment will yield a satisfactory return.

These may seem statements of the obvious. They are, but the fact is that these principles are unrecognized, or ignored, by many companies and the 'experts' who often advise them.

Over the years we observed one specific trend that continually baffled us. Many organizations increasingly invested vast sums in the purchase and implementation of extremely sophisticated customer management technology. Yet many of them failed to achieve even a small fraction of the benefits that had been promised when the investment decision was made. Despite this, hardware, software and consultancy suppliers continued to thrive, selling ever more complex solutions at ever higher prices.

It seemed to us that at the heart of the failure lay a lack of understanding of the principles described above. The belief seemed to be that a sprinkling of the magic dust of expensive technology was all that was required. Our opinion was, and remains, that while technology can be a very powerful enabler of many aspects of customer management, its introduction to a business that has not addressed the basics will almost always fail.

This book is about those basics.

We agreed to sell our consulting business at the end of 1999 and had both left by the spring of 2002 to pursue other interests – one of which was writing this book. We wanted to challenge some of the nonsense we had read and observed; to argue the case for a different approach based on our experience of what actually works – and what does not; and, most importantly, to provide all managers concerned with the management of customers and revenues with a fresh perspective.

The book is called *The Seven Myths of Customer Management* because in many organizations the basic tenets according to which customers are managed are founded more in mythology than reality. Of course everyone pays lip service to the need to treat customers well, everyone recognizes that they are important. But does everyone balance the need for a strong customer orientation with sound commercial common sense? It is sadly true that, despite the fact that only customers generate revenues and profits, many organizations remain unclear of how to unlock their potential value.

We hope you will find the book interesting and challenging. You may not agree with everything we say; we would expect nothing else. There is no single 'right' answer, or the definitive manual would have been written years ago. We simply offer our perspective gained from (far too many) years of observation and experience.

Paul Hawkes & John Abram
London
January 2003

Chapter 1

The Seven Myths of Customer Management

Debunking some Established Wisdom

It isn't that they can't see the solution. It is that they can't see the problem.
The Scandal of Father Brown, GK Chesterton

How many annual reports have you read in which the chairman or chief executive proclaims to shareholders about how 'customer led' the organization is, or is becoming? How many conferences have you attended where speaker after speaker provides advice and counsel on the merits of customer leadership? How many journals, magazines and books have you read that lecture senior executives on exalting in the primacy of the consumer and becoming customer led?

THE DANGERS OF CUSTOMER LEADERSHIP

It has become almost a mantra: to be led by customers is 'good' and is the way of the future, while to adopt any other posture is 'bad' and should be consigned to the past. This has been said so frequently, by so many eminent writers, thinkers and practitioners, that it has become woven into the fabric of business lore. Only a heretic would challenge the assertion – step forward the non-believers!

What Does Customer Leadership Mean?

We should take a moment to think about what being customer led means. There is no commonly accepted definition, so let us consider a range of statements with which you might agree. Being customer led requires listening to customers. It involves taking their complaints seriously and acting to ensure that similar problems are not repeated. It means recognizing and valuing customers for their importance to the business. It implies attempting to understand customer needs and then providing what they want, when they want it, through the channels of their choice, with the very highest standards of service. It means focusing on long-term customer satisfaction, even if this has a potentially damaging impact on today's business in terms of cost or lost revenues. It requires a restless dissatisfaction with the status quo and a continual drive to improve the customer's lot. In short, to be customer led is to recognize that the customer should be in prime position and to align the organization to achieve it.

Who Is Leading Whom?

The above are all sentiments with which any chief executive worth their salt would undoubtedly concur – or would they? If you tested some of the largest, most respected and successful companies in the world against these criteria, they would come up woefully short, often by design. Is Microsoft customer led? It listens to its customers and acts on their feedback, but only up to a point. Did the fact that its customers wanted unbundled web browsers make the slightest difference to Microsoft's strategy, or did it continue, as before, embracing its opportunity to maintain market leadership?

Is Sony customer led? The company makes and delivers first-class products and has efficient and effective after-sales service, but it is reputed to consult its customers only rarely during the development of entirely new product concepts. It has been said that it does not believe that customers have the vision, awareness or even perhaps the interest to be able to provide the company with appropriate insight into products of which they have no previous knowledge or experience.

Is Lloyds TSB customer led? The UK's largest and most profitable bank runs efficient operations; has invested millions in making its banking halls more attractive and customer friendly; and has led the charge in developing innovative new, added-value banking products for which customers are even eager to pay. On the other hand, it is quite prepared to cut the number of retail banking outlets by closing those that are unprofitable. It is content to charge its customers credit interest rates above those of its competitors; and it is sanguine about rationalizing its branch management structure to service customers through centralized telephone call centres.

Are these companies exceptions that prove the rule? Are they living in the past, with the market about to wreak its terrible revenge? Or do they have an alternative model that is not so much about being customer *led*, but more about being customer *focused*?

Adopting A More Commercial Perspective

Microsoft is prepared to listen to its customers if that does not result in its competitors gaining any advantage. Sony will continue to design and manufacture products for which there is no clear evidence of future market demand if it believes in them. Lloyds TSB is more than willing to risk the wrath of its customers if this ensures the bank's long-term growth and the maintenance of its pre-eminent market position. All these organizations have one ear on the market and one very carefully tuned into the needs of their shareholders. None is customer led, but all three are extremely customer focused. Is this distinction mere semantics or is there really a difference?

The respective management teams of Microsoft, Sony or Lloyds TSB would probably all, if pressed, agree with the sentiments behind being customer led. However, their first responsibility is to their shareholders, not their customers. Although they recognize that customers pay their salaries, they are not willing to accept the customer leadership credo at any cost. They are more than prepared to make tough decisions that sometimes create customer dissatisfaction, or exclude customers from the product design process, or result in higher prices or lower service levels, if this is to the long-term benefit of shareholders.

Being customer focused is different from being customer led because it overlays hard-edged commercialism. Customer focus includes all the elements of customer leadership, but only in as much as they facilitate or maintain competitive advantage. Customer-focused companies are quite prepared to make difficult decisions because they have a clear long-term vision for the enterprise, and have developed corporate and customer-management strategies designed to realize it. They recognize that not all customers are equally valuable, or potentially valuable, and they invest in their growth and development accordingly. They understand that customer satisfaction must, on occasion, be subjugated to commercial pragmatism. They acknowledge that not all customers are loyal, nor will they ever be so, and they manage them with one eye firmly fixed on both the profit and loss account and the balance sheet.

Most importantly, customer-focused companies recognize that the primary goal of any commercial organization is to create not satisfied customers, but satisfied owners. While they realize that the long-term interests of owners are unlikely to be served by ignoring customers or treating them with disdain, they have not allowed themselves to be misled into believing that the customer is always right. The customer is only right when the organization can afford it.

Successful organizations are *not* customer led. They might say that they are, because this is what analysts and shareholders want and expect them to say. But in reality it is a myth – customer focus is the goal to which they really aspire.

This book is about the achievement of customer focus. Its purpose is to dispel the myths and replace woolly thinking with commercial pragmatism, and to provide all managers involved in the management of customers with practical advice designed to maximize their profitability.

WHAT IS REALLY HAPPENING?

Never has there been so much advice for senior managers on how to manage their customers. Never have there been so many specialist magazines and journals to read; never more business books offering the latest quick-fix solutions; never more consultants fomenting dissatisfaction with the status quo and seeking to earn a crust by extolling the merits of their latest 'paradigm'.

Add to this the rapid development, and extremely skilled promotion, of a wide variety of innovative technologies and software systems, all of which guarantee a brand new set of insights and capabilities that promise the Holy Grail – including more customers acquired and retained, greater levels of customer satisfaction, lower costs and, of course, increased profits. All of these are fine in theory, but largely illusory in practice.

Over the last decade, organizations have professed to be more focused on the needs of their customers than ever before. Billions have been spent on customer relationship management (CRM), both in terms of technological support, marketing communications and staffing. Yet in most industries, and the overwhelming majority of companies, the old order still prevails. Product cross-sales rates are hardly different to those of 15 years ago. Despite massive investment, the High Street banks are still struggling to sell an average of one additional product to their current account customers, and the insurance companies envy their success!

Customers Are No More Satisfied or Loyal

Indeed, many commentators would argue that the growth and introduction of new technologies and routes to market have led to increasing levels of angst among consumers. Take as examples automated telephone menu and queuing systems, online servicing and direct communications, which are allegedly designed to build 'relationships' but, in reality, often confuse and alienate.

Despite the widespread introduction of many so-called loyalty schemes designed to stop customers from switching and provide tangible rewards, customer behaviour has hardly altered. If anything, the evidence suggests that such schemes have contributed to commoditization and educated an already fickle public to become even more promiscuous as customers.

What Is Going Wrong?

Why, despite huge investment and the best endeavours of many intelligent people, are customers not behaving as we want them to? Apart from sheer managerial incompetence (which, of course, cannot always be ruled out), there are probably two more common reasons: first, an over-reliance on platitudinous theories that are superficially attractive but also superficial in content; second, the adoption of theories that are sound but not understood in any depth by the managers charged with their implementation.

There has been little rigorous exploration of customer-management theories, processes and technologies and even less examination of the results of their implementation. Few companies have been prepared to 'come clean' about the return on investment they have achieved. As a result, a dangerous set of customer-management myths has emerged. Like all good myths they contain grains of truth, but these are often hidden by a mountain of nonsense.

MYTH 1: CUSTOMER RETENTION IS THE KEY TO INCREASED PROFITABILITY

It is during a recession that this particular myth gets trotted out with the greatest regularity. Times are hard and costs must be cut. The marketing and advertising budget is a tempting target and, after all, the received wisdom is that it costs much less to do business with existing customers than to acquire new ones. To make the message even more convincing, a relative cost ratio of 10:1 is often quoted as if it were a scientifically observable fact.

There is some truth in this argument, which lends it credibility. Mail-order traders have proven the essential validity of the assertion for nearly a century. All other things being equal, it will cost a great deal less to sell a product or service to an existing customer than to a new one. If you are looking to achieve the maximum return on your marketing investment, then this is as good a place as any to start. After all, your sales and marketing costs will be lower and existing customers, on whom you depend for ongoing profits, will be retained. Numerous problems arise, however, when you scratch beneath the surface and look at the ways in which this particular piece of 'wisdom' is applied.

Not All Customers Are Good Customers

The first realization, of course, is that not all things *are* equal. Within nearly every customer base there will be some who will buy practically anything offered to them. Unfortunately, there will probably be a far greater number who are more resistant, and many more still who will simply not buy, however attractive your product or proposition. Consider the new car purchaser who is determined to try a new marque, whatever your inducement; the current account customer who prefers to save with one of the new online market entrants for the greater convenience and in order to achieve a higher interest rate; the pension investor who yesterday purchased a new policy from a competitor in order to spread the risk.

But surely it must be more profitable to keep the customers you already have than to recruit new ones or, even more negligently, to allow them to slip away to competitors? Perhaps. The simple fact is that not all customers are the same. Not all customers are good customers. Not all generate profits equally. Some will be disproportionately profitable, while others may even destroy value. For example, some customers will require a greater volume of communication before they can be persuaded to repurchase. Others will use high-cost distribution channels because of their preference for face-to-face contact. Yet others will consume valuable resources in resolving their frequent service issues.

The Pareto principle – that 20 per cent of a phenomenon has 80 percent of its effects – exists and, in our experience, is often an understatement. The top 20 per cent of customers for one travel-related company with which we worked generated 96 per cent of total contribution to overheads. Conversely, the remaining 80 per cent of customers were responsible for a mere 4 per cent of the value. As can be seen from Figure 1.1, approximately 60 per cent

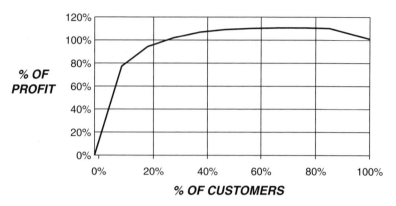

Figure 1.1   Travel company customer contribution
Reproduced with permission of Valoris Ltd

of the company's customers were actually unprofitable and were destroying value, yet all were being managed in exactly the same way, with exactly the same levels of investment. This was not a result of incompetence but rather ignorance of the composition and dynamics of the customer base; although for management to display such ignorance might well be regarded as incompetence. Consider for one moment the impact on this company's profitability when it became possible to match resources with value.

The maxim that 'all customers are good customers' is simply not true and can lead to dangerous, and expensive, mistakes. A more balanced perspective is required, one that considers the revenues and costs of both customer acquisition and retention – and overlays both with an understanding of performance and behaviour after the initial sale.

Ignore Customer Acquisition at Your Peril

Even if existing customers are proven to be more profitable, it does not mean that customer acquisition can simply be halted when times are hard. New customers acquired today are (or should be) the source of tomorrow's profits. The impact of abandoning customer recruitment is exacerbated by customer defections.

However good a company is at managing its customers, there will always be some who leave, even if only to move to a higher realm! Customers have a finite purchase lifetime, even though that might be measured in months or years. Consequently, any downturn in customer acquisition will flow through the organization to create a customer, and revenue, hole in the future. By the time the problem manifests itself, it is often far too late to take remedial action. The only options are to 'downsize' in order to reduce the cost base or accept the financial hit – expensive lessons that can have a terminal impact on a senior manager's career path.

Customer retention is a goal to which all should aspire – but not blindly and not to the exclusion of other customer development objectives.

MYTH 2: DIVESTING UNPROFITABLE CUSTOMERS WILL INCREASE PROFITABILITY OVERALL

Most organizations have a small number of customers who are generating a disproportionate amount of income; a relatively large number who are performing below the average; and some who are costing a great deal of money to retain and service.

Most 'experts' recognize the need to develop different strategies for the various customer value groups. Most also agree that companies should shed unprofitable customers, concentrating their effort and resources on those who contribute most to profitability. Such advice may seem self-evident and almost simplistic, but in fact implementing this kind of strategy can be fraught with difficulty. The credit card industry neatly illustrates some of the problems.

The Impact on Relationships

Consider a bank credit card issuer with a tranche of unprofitable cardholders who not only have satisfactory current account relationships but also, perhaps, hold a variety of mortgage, pension and high-value insurance products. Should the bank withdraw the cards? What would the fact that the bank is not prepared to adopt a customer-focused approach to managing the *totality* of the relationship say to these particular consumers?

The Impact on Allegiance

Consider a company that issues a credit card, but the card is not the primary relationship – a supermarket chain or utility company, for example. The impact on customer perceptions when the courtship of the acquisition process leads to disillusionment and divorce can visit irreparable damage on the core relationship. Is it inconceivable that previously loyal shoppers might change their grocery or energy allegiance following the forced withdrawal of their card facility, almost regardless of how much they previously used it? Will stemming losses on the card lead to lost profits elsewhere?

The Impact on Future Profits

Consider low-value cardholders who are attitudinally predisposed towards card usage and have lucrative potential earnings beckoning but, because of their life-stage or age, simply do not have the disposable income to demand high-value status. Ridding the company of such people at the start of their careers could jeopardize a lifetime of interest, cross-sales and card-usage income.

Consider the possible impact on new business acquisition of adverse word-of-mouth communication, or the damaging PR that could result from a low-value, but now very irate, journalist being disenfranchised!

What would be the long-term impact on press, consumer and analyst perceptions should Barclaycard, for example, voluntarily decide to forgo market leadership in card issuing because of a drive to maximize its short-term profitability? Would the ethical stance of the Co-operative Bank be compromised if cardholders were to react adversely to what they might perceive as unethical behaviour?

The Impact on Cost Structures

Finally, consider the possible ramifications of card withdrawal on cost structures and market positioning. While it is apparently sensible to downsize to avoid the costs of servicing and communicating with an unprofitable majority, the benefits may well be illusory. Depending on the way costs are apportioned, such cardholders may actually be making a valuable contribution to – largely fixed – overheads.

The financial logic of customer divestment appears unquestionable, but the practical realities of implementing this kind of strategy are considerable and there are a number of critical issues that need to be addressed prior to embarking on such a course.

Addressing the Critical Issues

Can you calculate the profitability of customers? Doing so presupposes the ability to identify not only revenues at an individual customer level (no mean feat in itself), but also those for all other non-core, or cross-sold, products. Using average revenue figures may be adequate for the purposes of analysis, but will be potentially dangerous when customer divestment is considered.

Can costs be allocated accurately at the same customer level? The fact is that some customers absorb more servicing resources than others and the use of average costs can distort the true profitability of individuals.

Has the possible impact on PR been assessed, as well as that on customer perceptions and intentions to repurchase? How would a downturn in word-of-mouth recommendations affect customer acquisition costs and volumes?

Can future purchase behaviour be forecast? Today's low- or no-value customer may well possess all the attributes and characteristics of tomorrow's high-value star. The low average purchase frequency, or annual expenditure, of a recent school or college leaver might be followed by high levels of use and the purchase of a wide range of other cross-sold products as both responsibility and disposable income increase.

Nevertheless, be careful. A major UK bank was considering the launch of a new account for the teenage market. It was clear that this would be a long-term investment, as the new account holders would undoubtedly lose money in the first few years of their relationship. Two separate, eminent firms of consultants were hired to help establish for how long the new young customers would have to remain with the bank for it to achieve an acceptable return on investment. One estimate was that the project would achieve the required returns within 12 years, a figure with which the bank was prepared to live. The second firm, however, concluded that the new accounts would never achieve the required level of profitability. As Nils Bohr said, 'prediction is very difficult, especially if it's about the future.'

Finally, how accurately can fixed costs be calculated and, more importantly, allocated? For an organization with a single product line such a question might appear facile, but for many others the allocation of indirect costs can make the difference between profit and loss at a customer or product level.

The disposal of unprofitable customers is self-evidently a 'good idea', but the benefits can be largely mythical. As with most business myths, the theory must be balanced by a plethora of other commercial considerations that frequently render the seeming elegance and simplicity of customer divestment an unacceptable risk.

MYTH 3: CUSTOMER SATISFACTION LEADS TO CUSTOMER LOYALTY

This particular myth is extremely pervasive and is arguably responsible for more wrong-headed decisions about the ways in which customers should be managed than any other. Again, the argument is deceptively seductive. The more satisfied customers are, the more they will buy. The more they buy, the longer they will continue to purchase. *Ergo*, customer satisfaction leads to customer loyalty.

There is, however, one simple yet major flaw in the logic. It is just not the case that satisfied customers will always buy more, or more frequently. Equally, it is an observable truth that not all loyal customers are satisfied. There is patently a relationship between satisfaction and customer loyalty, but there are enough examples where this is not the case to render the maxim a myth. Let's explore a few.

Are All Satisfied Customers Loyal?

All satisfied customers most certainly are not loyal or retaining customers would be a whole lot simpler, since a straightforward investment in making them happy would see the job done. To test the point, ask any group of friends or colleagues whether they are happy and satisfied with their car purchase. Post-purchase rationalization aside, most will agree that they are more than satisfied with their buy. However, ask the group whether they intend to buy the same model again and the answer will typically be very different. Satisfied, yes; loyal, no.

The same phenomenon can be seen in a wide variety of product and service categories. A successful family holiday with Thomas Cook may be followed by a trip booked through Lunn Poly, and vice versa. Customers who are more than satisfied with their local Esso petrol station will be equally content to visit a BP garage when they are out of the area. Someone who is happy buying their car insurance from Direct Line will see no reason not to purchase their home and contents insurance from the AA. British Airways frequent business travellers will see no irony in buying from easyJet when holidaying abroad at their own expense. Research has proved time and again that as many as 75 per cent of defecting customers are satisfied, or even very satisfied, with their former suppliers.

The reasons for customer defection are many. In the first place, 'defection' is probably the wrong word. It implies a strong emotional bond between customer and supplier. Many companies feel that they are able to establish such a relationship. They are usually (but not always) deluding themselves. There are very few products and services about which the majority of consumers feel strongly enough to establish true affinity.

Furthermore, much customer behaviour is serendipitous in nature. Buying habits are frequently driven by whim and chance, even for those purchases that should be entirely rational. In business-to-business markets rationality probably plays a greater role but, even here, purchase decisions are driven by many more factors than logic alone.

Are All Loyal Customers Satisfied?

Again, the answer is an obvious 'no'. Current account customers typically bank with the same organization, and frequently the same branch, throughout their working life, yet, with only a few notable exceptions, customer satisfaction with the banking industry remains extremely low. Many millions of people use the train network every day, despite their frustration and the ready alternative of a car or bus. And when was the last time anyone extolled the merits of their energy supplier over the dinner party table?

The relationship between satisfaction and loyalty can be seen in Figure 1.2. Only the Advocates, those customers who are both satisfied and loyal, can be relied on to deliver long-term value to the company.

One retail bank decided to quantify the behaviour and perceptions of its customers using this model and was disturbed by the results. The findings showed that just under half of its customers were satisfied with the service they received. More worryingly, however, only 35 per cent could be characterized as loyal, while a mere 20 per cent were both satisfied and loyal. Yet despite this damning evidence, customer attrition was stable and regarded as within historically acceptable limits.

Naturally, this does not mean that customer satisfaction is unimportant. Numerous studies have demonstrated consistently that

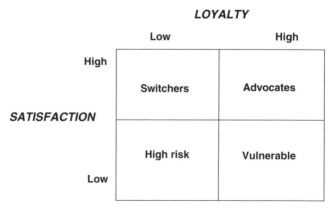

Figure 1.2   The satisfaction/loyalty matrix
Reproduced with permission of Valoris Ltd

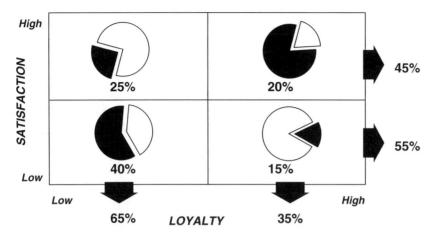

Figure 1.3   Satisfaction vs loyalty: retail bank
Reproduced with permission of Valoris Ltd

dissatisfied customers are less likely to buy again; that they tell their family and friends of the reasons for their dissatisfaction; and that it takes many more satisfactory service encounters to make up for one negative incident.

Just One Piece of the Jigsaw

So while customer satisfaction is an important component of customer retention, it is not a guarantee of loyalty. It is simply one piece of the jigsaw. Customer satisfaction is a comparatively small, albeit important, component of a much larger picture that determines whether the organization will grow and achieve consistent profitability.

Of equal importance are the inherent qualities of the product, staff satisfaction and morale, the perceived value that the product or service has for the customers that it serves and the purchase proposition.

MYTH 4: REPEAT PURCHASE IS THE SAME AS CUSTOMER LOYALTY

If customers continue to buy, then surely they can be regarded as loyal – right? Wrong! Customers buy from organizations for a wide variety of reasons, many of which have no relationship to 'loyalty' at all.

Consumers may select a company if it is close by, or uses particular distribution channels, such as the telephone or the Internet, that make it more convenient and accessible than its competitors. They may buy because they believe that the company offers the best price around, or because of the perceived difficulty in switching to another supplier. Or they may continue to buy even though they are completely disinterested in the product or service. Hard to believe? Perhaps, but how many people know that they really should change their mortgage to a cheaper supplier, but can't be bothered to do so? How many are saving each month in schemes that are producing below-average investment returns? How many are paying far too much interest on their credit card, despite the press regularly extolling the virtues of cheaper competitors?

Do we care – isn't the end result the same? We should care, because there are significant differences in likely levels of profitability between customers whose behaviour is driven by loyalty and those whose behaviour is a result of apathy, inertia or habit.

So What Is Customer Loyalty?

There are many different definitions of customer loyalty, but the one we prefer is: 'The combination of customer behaviours and attitudes that indicates brand or company preference, thereby maximizing customer lifetime value.' Loyalty implies faithfulness and allegiance, and it is indicative of behaviours that maximize customers' value over their purchase lifetime. Repeat purchase, on the other hand, is often short-term and indicative of transient behaviour that may, or may not, have any impact on enduring profitability.

Repeat buyers driven by convenience may be immediately tempted elsewhere if a new store opens nearer to where they live, or a previously preferred competitor begins to use the same distribution channels. Inert buyers may switch if environmental or life-stage issues change their priorities. Most people over 50 years of age begin to take a far greater interest in the value of their pension, for example, and the mortgage rate becomes significantly more important when marriage and babies are considered. Price-sensitive buyers will change at the drop of a hat if the product is offered more cheaply elsewhere. And the difficulties of switching will be negated if a competitor overcomes the barriers, or a service issue of sufficient magnitude prompts determined action.

You Can Buy Repeat Purchase, But You Can't Buy Loyalty

Short-term repeat purchase can frequently be stimulated by offers such as 'buy two and get one free', 'twelve months' subscription for the price of nine' or 'buy now and receive a free gift'. But all these techniques have hidden dangers.

Such practices are expensive. They can depress both margins and profitability. In addition, and perhaps more dangerously, they can condition customers to seek out these promotions and become more promiscuous. It is a habit that can become increasingly difficult to break because of the potentially detrimental, and immediate, impact on repeat purchase levels when such inducements are withdrawn.

Buying repeat purchase in this way can trigger a vicious sales promotion circle, as exemplified a few years ago by subscription wars in the US news magazine market. In order to maintain circulation to support advertising rates, the publishers offered an increasingly attractive, and increasingly expensive, array of rewards for both subscription and renewal. Unfortunately, the customers acquired in this way were significantly less loyal and therefore the value of the sales incentives escalated, while circulation market shares remained static. The profitability of all the players suffered accordingly.

This kind of promotion may also mean that customers will be buying for reasons only peripherally related to the product itself or the service surrounding its delivery. The company therefore becomes extraordinarily prone to the competitive threats posed by substitutes or replacements.

Behaviour such as this can enhance consumers' price sensitivity. By using price or incentives to gain repeat purchase, the consumers' purchase rationale is subtly shifted from the product to the offer. Consequently, your unique product and/or service benefits and points of differentiation may end up coming second to your competitor's two-for-one give-away.

Repeat Purchase Is Not Loyalty

Some practitioners will argue with these assertions. They will no doubt point to market test results that 'prove' that such offers increase the number of initial trials, that customer behaviour thereafter remains the same as ever, and that the overall result is therefore more profits. This may well be true in the short-term. However, it takes a very astute manager to make it work consistently, over protracted periods. Unless customer-acquisition targeting can be improved, or the product or service can be enhanced, or the proposition can be changed sufficiently frequently to maintain consumer interest, customer loyalty and longevity will gradually erode, necessitating ever-increasing sales inducements to maintain the same number of active customers.

Repeat purchase must not be confused with customer loyalty. They may look the same, but the differences are real and confusing them can have a profound influence on long-term customer profitability.

MYTH 5: ORGANIZATIONS SHOULD DEVELOP RELATIONSHIPS WITH THEIR CUSTOMERS

Rarely has so much nonsense been espoused by so many, so often and in so many places. In the attempt to build customer value, many organizations have determined, in their wisdom, that developing and nurturing relationships with their customers will cement loyalty and provide competitive advantage. Indeed, so pervasive has this idea become that a new acronym – CRM – has entered everyday business parlance. A brand new industry sector, grandiosely entitled Customer Relationship Management, has been built on the premise that becoming customer focused and developing customer relationships are mutually dependent and even synonymous activities.

CRM is frequently described as the means by which organizations can return to the values of the corner store, albeit using today's technologies to serve many thousands or even millions of customers. In the same way that corner store proprietors knew the names, individual needs and characteristics of their customers, so businesses can use modern technologies to build similar relationships, characterized by their understanding of and empathy with customers. In many cases the very word 'relationship' has become elevated to the pre-eminent goal, on the assumption that the development of closer customer relationships will increase customer retention and cross-sales success.

Relationships Can Be Beneficial

Of course, there are instances when building such relationships is a wholly appropriate and laudable strategy. Private banking for the affluent simply does not work unless there is a close relationship between the banker and his or her clients, for instance. To be successful, private bankers must understand each customer's income and wealth levels, their investment goals, their attitudes to risk, their income requirements and their retirement aspirations, as well as becoming a trusted and respected confidant. Similarly, wholesale grocery salespeople need to become very close to their key accounts in order to understand and anticipate their needs, adopt a proactive sales approach and provide a level of service and support that results in a recognized, and valued, source of differential competitive advantage. The relationship itself may also provide a very useful barrier to competitive encroachment; the deeper and broader this relationship is, the more likely it is that the customer will continue to buy and remain loyal.

There are, in fact, a wide range of different industries and sectors where the establishment of genuine relationships with customers is not only a critical strategy for long-term competitive success, it is also an essential component of day-to-day sales management. However, for many businesses the idea that they are building a relationship with the customer is an illusion based on arrogance and a profound lack of understanding of what makes customers think and act in the way they do.

Why, then, is the need to develop relationships with customers a myth? As with all of these myths, there is truth underlying the reality.

The private banker and the grocery salesperson are both successful because of the relationships they have developed to support a product or service that the customer values and, above all, with which they are deeply concerned. Therefore, the logic flows, if other businesses and managers can recreate the same depth of knowledge and understanding, commercial performance will be enhanced.

Unfortunately, for every fine example of the practical application of a relationship-building strategy, there are at least half a dozen where it is not the slightest bit appropriate – and will be costing the organization significant sums with little or no chance of any meaningful return on the investment made.

What Do Customers Want?

Do shoppers need, or desire, a relationship with a supermarket? Do frequent flyers want a relationship with an airline? Do regular savers value the relationship so vocally offered by their bank? Do consumers select a new car because of the relationship they have developed with the dealer's salesperson? Quite obviously, the overwhelming majority of customers do not. Supermarket shoppers prefer a wide selection of merchandise offered locally at reasonable prices in a pleasant environment with no queues. Frequent flyers want relevant network connections, a wide selection of convenient departure times and a record of punctuality. Savers want competitive interest rates, security and an appropriate level of access to funds. New car buyers want a competitive trade-in price, reinforcement of the brand's values, features and benefits – and a discount.

In fact, what customers want in all these instances is the right product, offered at a competitive price, available through the most convenient channels, at appropriate times and with a level of service that meets their needs. They most certainly do *not* want relationships; they find it hard enough to manage their existing relationships with friends, family and work colleagues. They do not want, do not have the time for and have no interest in developing relationships with commercial organizations.

What they do want is much simpler: products that work, live up to their sales pitch, represent value for money and are readily available; and service from staff who know what they are talking about and are accessible without undue delay. In short, they want what they have paid for. It's not sexy, is it?

Do Companies Really Want Relationships?

Do most organizations *really* want relationships with their customers, or would they simply prefer to acquire and keep profitable customers, and cost-effectively cross-sell to them as many other products and services as they can? The realization of these goals in today's mass-market world frequently demands a level of customer understanding and insight that was simply not available a decade or so ago. It means collecting and using appropriate information to analyse customer behaviour and communicate effectively; and it requires a level of technological support that will meet customer demands and minimize costs.

Relationships Should Never Be the Objective

The development of customer relationships may be an appropriate strategy or tactic in certain cases. It should *never* be the objective. In far too many cases, the expensive introduction of Customer Relationship Management infrastructure and software is simply a Band-Aid for woolly thinking and the absence of a well-conceived customer strategy that is, in turn, designed to support the corporate objective of increased shareholder value.

MYTH 6: ONE-TO-ONE MARKETING IS THE ULTIMATE GOAL

Isn't one-to-one marketing the ultimate example of customer focus? To listen to the many so-called gurus that promote this concept, one would certainly think so.

In this model, the organization collects and stores all relevant data about its customers, which it holds in centralized and easily accessible repositories that provide a consolidated view of customers and their purchase history and preferences. Customer histories and life-stages are tracked; individually tailored propositions are designed to respond to, or pre-empt, specific life events or behaviour; and personalized communications are sent, using the channels of customer choice, that recognize the uniqueness of each customer's circumstances and value.

A Segment of One

Each customer occupies a segment of one. No more grouping of customers into segments that don't quite fit. No more mass communications that are ill targeted, annoying and wasteful. No more customer propositions that are built around the financial value of the 'average' customer. And no more products offered at the wrong time to the wrong people. The ultimate business model – or is it?

If entrepreneurs with such a vision were starting a business today, with unlimited financial resources, multiple distribution channels and a sufficient volume of customers to justify the initial investment, then such a dream *might* be something to which they would aspire. Unfortunately, most of us live in a rather different world, populated by practical difficulties that render the dream exactly that: a dream.

Legacy Systems

Those organizations with the financial wherewithal, and the strategic intent, to consider one-to-one marketing will probably have legacy systems and infrastructure in place to service the needs of their existing customers, which will have been built, developed and enhanced over a great many years. Systems and architecture can always be changed and only a Luddite would suggest that progress should not be attempted. Nevertheless, the sheer scale of the change required to support one-to-one marketing should not be underestimated, nor should its cost. To justify improvements that may cost many millions to design, test, implement and manage requires a faith in customer performance enhancement that many decision makers find difficult to quantify with any certainty – especially in those industries where customer behaviour has not altered radically for many years.

Organizational Complexity

Even if the business case for the technology investment can be made and the investment is approved, there are issues relating to the day-to-day management of such potential complexity. Is it really possible to develop individually tailored propositions for each customer? Possibly, but in such a scenario the extent of personalization is likely to be minimal and may relate simply to price, delivery channel or something equally easy to adapt. Whether such adaptation will be meaningful for, and valued by, the customer is a moot point. More likely, the only manageable solution will be the design of a finite number of customer propositions, probably comparatively few, that will be employed to address the majority of customer situations – in other words, not segments of one but segments of many.

To be able to tailor propositions and communications to specific individuals requires the collection, storage and manipulation of a great deal of customer data. Only comparatively few companies have the resources and capabilities; those that do frequently complain about the additional, and often unmanageable, complexity that results from such data richness and the permutations of customer-management methods that it allows.

At a conference of senior managers from many different industries to debate customer-management issues of common interest, it was noticeable that those managers in industries that might be considered 'data poor', such as hotels, were bemoaning the difficulty they had in gathering customer information. At the same time, those in 'data-rich' areas such as banking were strongly questioning the cost and benefits of the mountains of data they had available to them.

Ballpark Budgeting

Budgeting is always difficult. Revenue and cost assumptions have to be developed based on how groups of customers are expected to behave in given sets of circumstances. Trying to do this in a one-to-one marketing environment is fraught with even greater difficulty. Imagine telling your Board that the budgeted sales are only a rough approximation because actual revenues will depend on individual customers' behaviour, trigger events and life-stages. Imagine saying that the ongoing marketing and servicing costs can only be ballpark figures because they will be determined by the number of people who exhibit the kinds of behaviour that stimulate the communications. To create greater certainty, until historical precedence can be used, it is necessary to be more specific about actions and quantities; and, of course, the more specific the plans become, the more they begin to resemble the old order.

The Opportunities for Error

Imagine the management complexity and the opportunities for error. All the possible permutations of offer, message, timing and channel have to be defined, specified, agreed, checked and controlled. *Things will go wrong*, not because people are incompetent, but simply because the complexity of true one-to-one marketing would require an army of expensive development and support staff.

Even if errors can be minimized, there are the complications of design. How will it be decided who receives which offers, when and through which channels? Only part of this equation can be truly led by customer preference and even then, someone must decide whether this preference can be allowed to overrule commercial economics. Suppose, for example, that a low-value customer professes a preference for face-to-face contact. Do you acquiesce in the hope that your empathy will be rewarded by enhanced long-term value, or do you use the telephone instead?

Management Challenges

How will the competing demands of different product-management groups be reconciled when both wish to promote their own products simultaneously to the same customers? Indeed, who will specify the objectives for the one-to-one marketing programme and on what basis will they be set? Who will determine, and how, which customers will be managed for growth, which will be simply retained at the lowest possible cost, and which will be cherished and nurtured?

The Impact on Testing

How will success be tested and measured when campaigns may run over many months, with comparatively few customers in each unique 'cell' and the resulting difficulties of establishing like-for-like control groups? Or will the rigours of testing be ignored, with all the consequent risk and potential damage to corporate development?

One-to-one marketing is a myth, not because it is impossible but simply because it is beyond the capabilities and resources of most organizations to plan, manage and deliver at an adequate return on investment. The concept is sound in theory, but in practice it requires a more pragmatic approach that balances cost with complexity and anticipated returns. Most companies are wrestling with the ability to calculate customer value, to understand customer life-stages and purchase trigger points. Many are only just coming to grips with customer-segmentation models that truly drive marketing and servicing resource-allocation decisions. Few are really employing these models to specify discrete and measurable objectives, strategies and plans that recognize value, potential value and customer characteristics or preferences. Fewer still are imposing rigorous testing and learning disciplines that accurately measure the success, or otherwise, of their customer-management activities. Until a tick can be placed in all of these boxes, one-to-one marketing will remain an unattainable dream for the vast majority of companies.

MYTH 7: TECHNOLOGY IS THE PRIMARY ENABLER OF CUSTOMER FOCUS

Of all the myths of customer management, this is possibly the most misleading and has certainly been the most expensive. It is undoubtedly true that, particularly over the last two decades, the technologies available to manage customers more efficiently and effectively have multiplied. Twenty years ago, the concept of using a database to store and manage customer data for marketing activities was in its infancy. Fifteen years ago automated call distributors (ACDs) revolutionized the ways in which customers could be managed on the telephone, for sales or servicing purposes. Ten years ago, the web was almost the sole preserve of academics and researchers.

Now the launch of new technologies, or new software packages designed to take advantage of them, appears to be an almost everyday occurrence. There are new tools for analysis, campaign management and personalization. There are new systems for data warehousing, e-commerce and mobile telephony. All promise better ways of managing customers to improve customer focus, increase revenues and/or decrease costs. All are marketed and sold enthusiastically and professionally by a whole new breed of CRM experts, primarily from IT or systems backgrounds. And the major international management consultancies have not been slow to realize the sales potential from this new revenue source. Many have entered into partnerships with the larger IT vendors to market their products, albeit under an assumed cloak of objectivity, and to reap the huge fees that arise from the subsequent need for systems integration.

The Emperor's New Clothes?

All of these groups have been very successful. Over the last decade, IT directors have enthusiastically adopted the latest pieces of kit. Chief executives have been seduced by the promised commercial benefits from greater market orientation and customer revenues. Marketing directors have propounded the cause of improved customer focus and the flexibility that such systems and technologies offer. Have cross-sales ratios improved? Have marketing and customer-servicing costs been slashed? Are customers happier and more satisfied? Have they all been duped?

The simple truth is that in the vast majority of cases few, if any, of the promised benefits have materialized. Millions of pounds have been spent; old systems have been discarded; new organizational structures have been introduced; companies are swimming in oceans of new-found customer data – but customer performance remains firmly rooted in the models of the past. Why? Because organizations have been seduced into buying the latest gizmos with no understanding or appreciation of what they would actually do differently once they got them up and running.

Challenging the Art of the Possible

In earlier times, the organizational order of things was well established. Chief executives were responsible for developing corporate strategy. Marketing, sales and customer service directors were charged with designing customer-related strategies for their own functional areas of specialism. IT directors were typically asked to provide the architecture and software support required to realize the individual, and largely separate, goals of the various customer managers.

However, CRM systems and technologies broke the mould. Two things happened. Because these promised a holistic perspective on customers and the ways in which they might be managed, their introduction became a cross-functional issue involving all business disciplines. So, in seeking an appropriate champion, most chief executives looked towards the IT director as in-house expert.

Concurrently, it could be seen that many of the new technologies were changing the art of the possible. The Internet was not developed from its early incarnation in response to customer demand, but it did facilitate the creation of new business models, and new ways of marketing, selling and servicing customers. Wireless Application Protocol (WAP) promised the opportunity to add value, differentiation and new revenue streams for the mobile operators. Smart cards enabled the development of the electronic purse, a replacement for cash, which might have changed the economics of the banking industry.

Unfortunately, however, successful new web-based business models have proven thin on the ground. As yet, nobody seems yet able to create and supply WAP content for which a significant number of mobile phone users are willing to pay an economic price, and the electronic purse is a product desperately in search of a market. Nevertheless, this is to be wise after the event and does not detract from the central point that almost overnight, new technologies enabled those with the knowledge of their capabilities to lead the corporate and customer investment agendas.

Fear and Uncertainty

The situation was compounded by fear and uncertainty: the fear and uncertainty of being left behind by more innovative competitors; and of not being perceived by customers or investors as sufficiently customer focused. Both were very real, but resulted in a headlong rush into new technologies and systems for which there were often no strategies or plans for their commercial exploitation. Customer managers were then asked to retrofit their plans around IT systems that were bought for their own sake, rather than to resolve clearly articulated business problems or take advantage of identified market opportunities. Unsurprisingly, the end result has been confusion, perceptions of squandered corporate resources and infighting between IT directors and the very customer managers that the systems were initially designed to support.

The Need for Vision

The benefits of new technologies are there to be had, but only if their introduction is driven by an appropriate vision and objectives, a vision and objectives that are realistic and geared to generating greater profitability.

Technology is *not* the primary enabler of customer focus. Greater customer focus comes from having clear and commercially considered customer-management objectives, strategies and plans to which everyone ascribes. Technology, and technologists, must naturally play a significant role, but they must not lead the charge in isolation.

A DIFFERENT APPROACH

Quite simply, a different approach is needed: one that appreciates the importance of customers as the only source of revenues and profits; but one that also understands the critical importance of hard-nosed and practical commercialism. Where should we start?

Chapter 2

Testing the Water
Understanding Where You Are Today

Much learning does not teach understanding.

Heraclitus (540–480 BC)

A major mobile phone company used to offer subscribers an add-on service of five free text messages per day, in return for a one-off charge. Then, for reasons best known to itself, the company decided to reduce the number of free daily messages from five to three. A customer (maybe one of many) complained that the change was directly contrary to the way the service had been advertised when it was sold in one of the company's own retail outlets, where it had been described as 'Five free text messages for life'.

The response to the customer's rather mildly expressed letter dismissed the complaint as entirely unwarranted, ending with a curt statement to the effect that any attempt to continue the correspondence would merely result in the company restating its position. However, the customer was not so easily dissuaded from pursuing the fundamental issue that the company was reneging on a clear obligation to which it had previously committed.

The correspondence continued over several weeks, during which the organization repeatedly refused to entertain the customer's complaint, insisting time after time (notwithstanding the threat of litigation) that this was completely without merit and that its own position was absolutely final.

Suddenly, however, the company changed its stance, conceded to the customer's demands and reverted to the previously promised five free daily text messages. The letter in which it accepted defeat concluded as follows: 'I trust this response is satisfactory and shows that [company], as an award winning service provider, do value our customers and their opinions.'

Ignoring the grammar (or lack of it), did its writer genuinely believe that the customer would feel positively inclined towards a company that had to be threatened with court action before accepting it was in the wrong? Whether that final paragraph was blindly and thoughtlessly selected on the word processor or was a genuinely held belief of the author, it is hard not to conclude that this is a business that lacks true customer focus.

Of course, this anecdote may be unique and entirely unrepresentative, although the existence of various websites set up by a plethora of angry customers would seem to indicate otherwise. The chances are that, to allow such a situation to occur, the business exhibits a mindset that is either arrogant, ignorant or both. It's a safe bet, however, that it also has research reports by the yard 'proving' just how wonderful it is to its customers.

In that, it is not alone. Many companies believe that they are closer to their customers than they actually are. They believe that their customers admire and respect them when the reality is often that, at best, they are merely tolerated. They continue to lose customers even though their corporate measures regularly show that high standards of service delivery are being achieved.

Where does this disconnect between perception and reality arise? How can it be that companies and managers so often fail to form a realistic view of how they are seen by their customers? The reasons are both complex and simple: complex in that there is usually a combination of factors that combine to prevent an organization seeing clearly the realities of its actual position; simple in that the things that are most often wrong, from a customer perspective, are almost always basic errors that can be fixed with relative ease and at modest cost.

There is a widespread misconception that customer focus means conceding to every customer demand and request, almost irrespective of cost. This is wrong – and patently not commercially sound. What customer focus does mean is understanding enough about customers to be able to deliver a proposition (including product, positioning, service etc.) at a price the customer is prepared to pay, and at a cost that allows the business to grow long-term shareholder value.

Developing customer focus is not easy and can be extremely time consuming. It may involve setting new goals, retraining staff, designing new processes, introducing new systems, developing new products and customer propositions, or adding new distribution channels. And the job is never done. Markets evolve and customers become more sophisticated and demanding. New competitors enter the market and existing competitors launch new initiatives. Governments change regulatory frameworks and new technologies alter the art of the possible. Maintaining an organization's focus on its customers therefore requires ongoing commitment.

Nevertheless, the prize is worth the effort. The customer-focused company intimately understands the attitudes and needs of its customers and prospects. It develops products and services that are attractive and relevant. It markets and sells to those customers at times that are appropriate, through channels that are preferred, with prices and propositions that are persuasive and are perceived to represent value for money. Most importantly, however, it invests in customers in accordance with their current and potential value. The customer-focused organization recognizes that it exists to maximize shareholder value and that being nice to customers is simply a means to an end, not an end in itself. The first step on the road must be to develop the customer understanding and intelligence required to enable those difficult investment decisions to be made.

To stand any chance of success, a company must have sensitive antennae that can pick up the often very weak signals transmitted

by customers. These signals are frequently confusing and sur-
rounded by interference and noise. The key is to be able to tune in
to the real messages and act accordingly. By the time the signal is
strong enough to be heard clearly, it may be too late.

So what can done – cheaply, quickly and easily – to enhance the
understanding of customers significantly?

PICKING UP CUSTOMER SIGNALS

Later we will discuss formal methods, such as market research, that
can be used to develop a better understanding of what customers
think and believe and why they behave as they do. First, let's consider a powerful approach to gaining the insight that will help your
business make truly customer-focused decisions. This approach
costs little, but can prevent your firm stumbling into that fantasy
world where perception and reality become divorced – where the
staff (particularly at the top of the business) have only the vaguest
notion of what customers really think and how they behave.

Listening Hard

Listening may not seem like much of a solution, but it is. Listening
is the key to picking up those weak and often confusing trans-
missions from customers that, if tuned into, understood and acted
on, can make a vast difference to your organization's ability to maximize customer value. However, listening is a skill. It needs to be
practised, which means finding the opportunity to do it a lot. Ask
yourself this: how much time do you spend with customers – and
how often? What do you do differently as a result of meeting or
talking to customers? What about your colleagues?

Sadly, most managers spend far too little time with the people
who ultimately pay their salaries – their customers. There are a few
notable exceptions of companies where everyone from the boss
down regularly gets involved. MBNA, an American-owned credit
card issuer, has a simple but powerful phrase above every doorway
of its offices worldwide: *'Think of yourself as a customer.'* Every
manager, up to the level of vice-president and regardless of job

function, must spend four hours a month answering customers' phone calls. Although senior managers are spared the hot seat, they are not exempt and have to listen into calls for the same time in a purpose-built room.

Sometimes, even when such laudable practices are employed, the process can become routine and be followed by rote, rather than because the participants really appreciate the value it can bring.

Why do most managers find it so hard to justify taking, or making, the time? Unfortunately, arrogance is all too often at the heart of the matter. Many believe that they are rather too important to have to bother. They won't usually admit this, but will claim that they are too busy. This is simply illogical. The return on investment from listening to customers can be immense. It provides insights and understanding that can influence all areas of decision making.

Disappointingly, many senior managers regard customers collectively as a source of revenues and profit, and singly as a source of complaint and cost. Customers are not seen as individual people with differing values, personal hopes, aspirations and fears, but as a homogenous corporate resource that has been purchased, in much the same way as the office furniture or a new warehouse.

The Customer/Management Disconnect

There are only a very few large businesses where the customers are actually like the people who serve them. For most consumer-focused organizations, management is divided from the overwhelming majority of its customers by education, income and sometimes social class. It is highly unlikely that a company with, say, two million customers and a turnover of several hundred million pounds a year will be managed by people who share the same values as the customers it seeks to satisfy. They will not think and behave alike, nor will they have the same fears and aspirations. Yet it is the customers who pay the bills, who allow the management to build the business and grow shareholder value. Anything that managers can do to gain an understanding of these people must be worthwhile. Every manager must make the time – it's part of the job.

The now retired, middle-class and well-educated managing director of a market-leading direct-to-consumer business was faced one day with the inescapable realization that he had a handful of named, and readily identifiable, very high-value but very down-market customers who were responsible for generating many thousands of pounds in sales each year. It was suggested that he might like to host a dinner for them. It was further suggested that not only would this cement their purchasing habits, but it would also generate greater insight into a very valuable, small and discrete customer segment. He was horrified by the idea and, needless to say, the restaurant remained unbooked.

Listening to customers is not something that can happen once a year, or over the dinner table. It has to become a habit, a part of the way the business is run. Take home some randomly chosen letters or e-mails from customers. Spend a few minutes every now and then listening to customers' telephone calls. Sit in on focus groups or even, if you are feeling really brave, find a way to meet some customers face-to-face.

Meeting Customers

When Marcus (later Lord) Sieff was running Marks & Spencer in its heyday, he was renowned for the frequency with which he visited the stores – particularly on Saturdays when he could do so without neglecting his workload at the Baker Street head office. During his visits he listened to his local staff and to his customers. What is more, he acted on what he discovered. Once, on visiting a newly opened store in Brussels, he was told that a particular line of ladies' nightwear would not be bought by any self-respecting Belgian woman of taste and style. Conversations with the store manager confirmed that this popular UK product was, indeed, not selling. It was removed from the store the following day. Of course, that may or may not have been the right decision but, if nothing else, it convinced the staff that Marcus Sieff was listening.

Anecdotal Evidence

However diligently anyone listens to customers, reads their letters or meets them face-to-face, the sample will nearly always be a small proportion of the whole, particularly in a mass-market consumer business. Managers will often say that to make decisions on the basis of what is, essentially, anecdotal evidence is flawed, so what is the point of taking all that time to listen in the first place? Clearly, no business should be run solely by observing the whims and behaviour of a few customers. This is obviously merely one of the sources of information available, but it is a source of great potential insight and can provide the input that allows the hard data to be interpreted and understood.

Someone Else's Problem

Even when the intellectual argument is won, many managers still fail to take personal responsibility for listening and talking to customers. Why? Because they employ a marketing department and a sales force. Surely, that is what *they* should be doing? After all, these teams are paid to be responsible for understanding customers. Such thinking is nevertheless flawed. Second-hand information is always a poor substitute for the real thing, particularly when the source of the data may very well have a vested interest in putting a favourable spin on what is being said.

In addition, how often do the people in your marketing team themselves meet customers? It is a worrying trend that many marketing staff these days fulfil their roles in glorious isolation from the people about whom their job should revolve. This isolation is bred from the same flaw of arrogance, and sometimes a misplaced belief in the omnipotence of market research.

Of course, the sales team will be spending time with customers. Isn't their feedback sufficient? No, it's not. There simply can be no substitute for hearing what customers have to say at first hand.

Everybody's Problem

Could the need to meet and listen to customers be restricted to the boss and those on his or her team with customer-related responsibilities? That is better than nothing, but far from ideal. Customers are everyone's business. Understanding who they are, how they think, how they act, what they like and dislike will help everyone make decisions that are more insightful and customer focused –

decisions that will have the greatest possible chance of growing shareholder value because they recognize the requirement to balance the needs of customers with those of the company. For a business to maximize the value hidden in its customers, the whole organization must think and act in a truly customer-focused manner. Encouraging as many of your colleagues and staff as possible to spend time with customers on a regular basis is one of the most powerful ways of getting this message across.

BUSINESS-TO-BUSINESS CUSTOMERS

In a business-to-business environment the need to listen to what customers have to say is every bit as great as in a consumer-oriented firm. Fortunately, a higher level of customer contact is much more common. Yet many simple mistakes can still be observed that would, if corrected, greatly enhance insight and understanding and, at minimal cost, significantly improve decision making.

For most organizations selling to business customers, the sales force will typically be the primary point of customer contact. In a well-run sales operation there will be mechanisms in place to capture and collate customer feedback. Leaving aside the constant claim that prices are too high (has there ever been a sales force that couldn't sell more if only the prices were lower?), this feedback can be extremely misleading. Why? Because sales people are human – they prefer to spend their time with people they like and with whom they get on.

It is all too easy for salesperson and customer alike to drift into a relationship of mutual mediocrity in which both parties are apparently getting what they want, all is well and comfort zones are not threatened. This type of relationship may well bring in the business today, but is unlikely to generate the warning signals that will ensure the continued success of the business in the longer term.

Listening for Bad News

To pick up the appropriate signals from customers it is necessary to talk and listen not only to 'friends', but also to the disgruntled and the difficult. Lapsed customers and those with whom the firm has never done business must also be heard. To expect the sales team to do this is probably unrealistic, but even if they do, there is still a need for the whole company to engage in the listening process.

Listening has to start at the top. Senior managers must take the lead in being prepared to meet customers. Many chief executives are all too often shielded from the reality of what their customers actually think and believe. Barriers are erected when they are kept away from customers who have something less than positive to say, or when they meet in a context that makes it difficult for a customer to speak openly.

A Board director of one of the UK's leading public companies accompanied the head of his key account team on a series of meetings with major customers. The feedback was generally positive and constructive. Just two weeks later, the same Board director was at a charity dinner where, by chance, he met one of the customers he had seen a fortnight before. It was a case of *in vino veritas* as a picture emerged of weak account management, a lack of responsiveness and a general feeling of dissatisfaction and unhappiness that had been growing for some time. Furthermore, detailed probing with other customers revealed a similar, although not universal, picture. Even though the director had made the time and effort to meet the customer, mutual mediocrity, combined with a natural sense of courtesy, had conspired to prevent the customer from challenging the key account manager in front of one of his directors, creating a dangerously misleading impression of the true situation.

Size is *Not* Everything

Sometimes the company's chosen business strategy will also erect a barrier to hearing the whole story. Many business-to-business strategies are built around focusing attention on those customers who have produced the most business in the immediate past. The inclusion of a customer on a key accounts list is almost universally driven by historical volume data. Little thought is given to the customer's profitability or potential. This approach is rather like steering a boat by looking at its wake. Most of the time it works well: the boat can be kept in a straight line and even manoeuvred on to a different heading. The danger lies in failing to recognize the reef that lies ahead.

If customer contact is only to be with the 'usual suspects', the established group of high-value customers who regularly bring in the business, the opportunity to understand how the market is changing, what is new and what is different may well be missed.

One major player in the corporate insurance market fêted its largest broker customers, spending time, effort and resources on meeting key personnel, developing deep and personal relationships, anticipating and satisfying their needs. Unfortunately, size was not everything. When it was proven that it was in fact the very smallest brokers who were responsible for most of the company's profit, its key account management programme had to be completely rethought.

Even when it can be shown that large customers are unprofitable, many organizations cling to customer size as a comfort blanket and are reluctant to consider a wider perspective. This does not mean, of course, that large customers should be ignored. It does mean that they will probably only provide part of the picture and that positive steps must be taken to listen to as wide a cross-section of other customers as possible.

Ignoring Face-to-Face Dialogue

One of the world's largest technology businesses was embarking on planning a new strategy for its UK servicing operation, a business that in its own right would have been large enough to be included in the FTSE 250 list. The company was an expert and extensive user of research and ran, among other programmes, a comprehensive tracking study to measure the satisfaction of its business partners, who represented its primary route to market. One constant theme that emerged from the research was that it was excessive! The distributors felt that they spent too much time completing surveys.

However, when the strategy planning team started work, one of the first things they wanted to do was, not surprisingly, talk to these distributors to gain a better understanding of how they saw their markets changing over the coming years. The request was initially turned down by the head of the service business, on the basis of the research feedback already achieved. Any further approaches to business partners were, it was believed, likely to cause real problems. Following some painful negotiation, the project team gained agreement to visit a very small number of distributors for face-to-face discussions. Furthermore, no one from the service division was to be present.

What emerged was a revelation. As one of the distributors visited said: 'At last, someone is asking me the questions I want to answer. I complete the service standard surveys every month and I know that the information is important. But I never get a chance to talk about the things I want to discuss – it's always their agenda and never mine.'

To the great credit of the company concerned, it listened hard, immediately expanded the programme of interviews and gathered information that was central to the development of its new strategic direction. Even those companies that are assiduous in their efforts to understand their customers can get it horribly wrong if they ignore face-to-face dialogue.

WHAT RESEARCH DOES NOT TELL YOU

Another excuse for not making the time to listen is that the company already has an extensive body of research that reveals everything it needs to know about its customers. This research has been carefully designed and skilfully executed at great expense to answer, with precision, questions about customer attitudes, needs and future intentions.

Nuance

Clearly, research plays a vital role in providing the essential data on which decisions can be based. But it rarely provides the subtlety of input that can be gained from talking and, more importantly, listening to customers. Filtering inevitably takes place between what customers said when questioned and the final presentation to senior management. The interviewer or moderator records the findings, which are then aggregated, summarized, debated and perhaps presented to the market research team, which in turn presents to the marketing management. Eventually, a report emerges that may, or may not, be believed and acted on. This filtering does not necessarily invalidate the research, but it does frequently hide the subtle and important nuances of the customers' feedback.

Relative Importance

One particular failing of much research is that it simply does not accurately offer to the commissioning company a vivid picture of the customer's perceptions of the relative importance of the firm and its products and services. In most research projects it is inevitable that the company, product or service being studied will be at the front of the research subject's mind, simply by virtue of participation in the research. So for the duration of the interview or discussion, the topic assumes a high degree of importance. As a result, all too often the attitudes and opinions expressed become credited with a status that belies reality, which can lead managers into believing that customers (both existing and potential) are much more interested in the firm's proposition than is actually the case.

Even when the research incorporates trade-off analysis to identify customers' priorities, the options are usually between elements of the product and service. Is feature A more important than feature B, and by how much? If, on the other hand, companies were to ask which is more important, feature A or getting home in time to watch *Coronation Street*, they might discover that their so-called customer relationships are rather less robust than they had previously imagined.

Customer Profitability

Research cannot predict the future with much confidence, nor can it compute customer profitability. Only trading data can reveal which customers are creating value and which are destroying it. Research may provide some indication of potential purchase intentions, but even then its value is questionable. The greatest learning about likely behaviour does not come from what customers tell you they will do, but what they (or people like them) have actually done; and data analysis is typically more useful than research for this particular task.

Sample Design

Research is only as good as its sample design. Therefore, unless the organization already has a robust value-based customer-segmentation model in place, it is likely that a sample will be based on criteria such as age, geographic location and historical purchase patterns. This means that it will comprise customers of differing values, potential values, opinions, attitudes and life-stages. The result will be a picture of the average customer – *but the average customer does not exist*. Attempting to base any customer-focus programme on the needs of this mythical creature will satisfy nobody and, inexorably, result in expensive failure and disillusionment.

Research is insufficient on its own. Successful decision making is about synthesizing as much relevant data as can be gathered and then making judgements on the best, or least worst, course of action. The data alone will not make the decision for you. If your judgement is to be sound, the data needs to be rich – not merely in volume and accuracy, but also in depth and diversity. Listening and talking to customers can provide these attributes. It can add different shades of meaning to the hard research results. It can make the bald facts presented by your management reports come alive and become more meaningful. Sometimes, it can even give the lie to the perceived wisdom that many firms have misled themselves into believing over many years.

Customer research is extremely valuable. It can provide insights into behaviour and motivation that cannot be achieved with other methods of investigation. Nevertheless, it is typically insufficient for the customer-focused chief executive. A broader, more comprehensive picture is required, one that provides a deeper understanding that can only be achieved by meeting with, and talking to, customers.

NEW TECHNOLOGY, NEW DANGER

The Internet is proving a customer-management channel that, in some important ways, differs from all others. Leaving aside the more outlandish (and, fortunately, now mostly discredited) claims about a so-called new economy being created from a fundamental shift in customer behaviour, there are some aspects of doing business on the Web that are particularly challenging. The most significant of these, in the context of this chapter, is the remoteness of the customer.

Physical Remoteness

Today it is possible for, let's say, a software provider in the Far East to supply its products to customers anywhere in the world. Payment is taken electronically through one of the universal payment systems, such as Visa or MasterCard, and the product itself is delivered via the Web. Many of these businesses are attempting to come to grips with the challenge of their remoteness by using the very technology that allows them to be so remote in the first place. Herein lies the danger. The desire to use sophisticated technology seems to take precedence over thinking through the customer experience. Two examples that may seem all too familiar illustrate the point.

A website that allows users to download Internet security products also has a problem-solving feature to help sort out any issues with the installation and use of the software. If customers have cause to use this facility, they receive an e-mail asking for feedback. They are asked to rate the company's service elements and to provide commentary in a box for free-form text. However, any customer who responds with negative comments, stating that the problem has not been resolved, hears nothing and is left feeling as if the desire for customer feedback is actually limited to the wish for adulation, that complaints are really not welcome and that the company is not at all serious about satisfying its customers' needs.

Many major airlines allow their frequent flyers to manage their reward points over the Internet. If everything works well, it's a great service. However, if there is a problem with a missing claim or an incorrect points allocation, many of these sites leave the customer feeling not merely isolated, but positively unloved. A customer of one such airline recently had to write on four separate occasions to obtain the reward points due. The website could not be used because the airline wanted copies of documents. Not one of the letters produced so much as an acknowledgement of receipt, either by post or e-mail, let alone an apology for the inability of the airline to do what it had promised. The customer commented, 'It was as if I had ceased to exist because I stepped outside their circle of technology.'

Mental Remoteness

Many of these technology-driven programmes appear to be constructed without any input from people within the business who have any experience of meeting, talking and listening to customers. Sometimes the impression is created that no one has taken the time to think about how the technology will be used in real life. There are at least two well-known credit-card issuers in the UK who use automated phone technology to manage the reporting of lost or stolen cards and the issue of replacements. At one point in both companies' processes, customers are asked to input their credit-card number using the phone's touch pad. Should the number not be to hand (because the card is lost or stolen, perhaps), there is no option to transfer to an operator. It is therefore impossible for many people to report a serious servicing issue that could result in costly fraud.

This chapter began by questioning how often senior managers met with, talked to and listened to customers. When was the last time your head of IT or the people leading your technology project teams did the same? Arguably, it is even more important that these people, whose efforts are often primarily focused on cost reduction and removing expensive customer contact points, should have an understanding of how their efforts will feel to the customer. The process maps will show *what* is happening, but cannot replicate what it *feels like* to be a customer. Without that insight, major errors of judgement can often be made.

SUBSTITUTING BENCHMARKING FOR THOUGHT

Some years ago, the idea of benchmarking key aspects of business performance against competitors and companies with similar operating challenges started to become a popular management tool, leading to the concept of becoming a 'best-in-class' player.

One aspect of this trend was hugely valuable. It persuaded managers that their business was not unique and that there were lessons to be learned from other firms in terms of operational techniques and management styles. Enabling companies in any industry to widen their horizons and recognize that they do not have the answer to every business challenge is important and can add significantly to shareholder value.

For some – particularly in the financial services sector – this was a revelation. A favourite retort to those trying to persuade firms in the sector to study the lessons of other industries was: 'Look, selling a pension is not like selling baked beans, you know.' A typical response, which was guaranteed to spark a lively debate, was: 'You're right. Selling baked beans is much harder – those firms don't know who their customers are; and they rely on someone else, who is responsible for thousands of alternatives, to present, promote and sell a product that has no impact on the future wealth and security of the customer. Whereas you . . .'

The Urge to Be 'Best'

However, benchmarking also has a major failing if it is not managed with finesse. Sadly, even in a business world that is perhaps more rational than at any time in the last 30 years, macho management is still a common attribute. The biggest market share, the fastest rate of growth, the most ambitious acquisitions all seem to be watchwords for some business leaders. It is hard not to feel that some (and arguably too many) management teams are more motivated by the thrill of the chase than by commercial common sense. Of course, these same people are usually very eloquent and persuasive, and will deliver the arguments in favour of their chosen course of action with great conviction. Benchmarking all too often plays up to these competitive instincts as management focuses on

being 'the best' at each of the measures identified as business critical during the benchmarking process.

This misses the point. Few benchmarking exercises go so far as
to demonstrate whether or not the chosen performance indicators
are those that have the greatest impact on customers and their subsequent buying behaviour. Thus, being the best at things that do
not really matter may feed the egos of management, but will not
improve customer faithfulness or increase shareholder value.

Figure 2.1 illustrates the concept. Whenever a company is performing well on matters of little importance to the customer, it may
well be that it is over-investing in that particular process or feature.
Conversely, when customers indicate the matter to be important
yet performance is poor, it will often be a sign that the organization
should be taking remedial action.

While benchmarking is often useful, it is highly unlikely that it
will provide all the answers. Only by talking to customers directly,
through research or other means, can a robust view of customer
importance and company performance be achieved.

A white-goods manufacturer took part in a benchmarking exer-
cise with five other firms from different industries, but with several
commercial elements in common. One of the areas examined was
after-sales service, where it was shown that some had very slick
processes for measuring the time it took to respond to initial service
call-outs. This immediately became one of the manufacturer's new

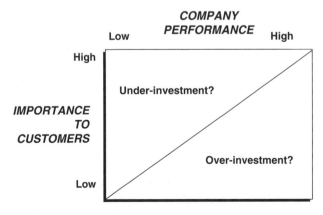

Figure 2.1   Importance vs performance

performance indicators and, over a period of six months, significant time and money were spent on reducing response times until they were 'best in class'. Sadly, it was subsequently shown that, while the initial response time was of interest to the customer, of much greater importance was having a guaranteed time for the service call. Customers would far rather have waited 48 hours for the service visit if they could be guaranteed that it would be at a specific time, rather than at any time during the day at the manufacturer's convenience.

It could be argued that this is not the fault of benchmarking, but of poor management. That is true, up to a point. However, in this case, benchmarking precipitated a chain of analysis that was directed towards delivering best-in-class performance, irrespective of the customer's needs and attitudes. In other words, this was not customer-focused decision making.

Maximizing Customer Value

Being customer focused does not mean being the best, the biggest or the fastest. It means doing whatever it takes to maximize the value of the customer and, therefore, the business. This may actually be achieved by being demonstrably worse than other firms in some areas of performance, if such activities do not create, or detract from, long-term value. One only has to think of the several very successful discount retail chains in diverse areas such as food, clothing and linens to realize that for some customers, having the best store locations, the fanciest layouts or the broadest range of stock would be poor substitutes for fantastically low prices.

Yet again, the issue becomes one of customer understanding: having the necessary knowledge to interpret the raw data from research and management information with creativity and subtlety.

TEN WAYS TO GAIN REAL CUSTOMER INSIGHT

Most companies fail to spend enough time listening to their customers and even when they do, in meetings, answering phone calls or reading research reports, what is heard is often not the full story.

The subtleties hidden within the customer feedback are frequently missed or ignored.

So here are some specific activities that need not cost significant amounts, but are quick and easy to implement and will dramatically improve the quality of your customer understanding and decision making. But be warned: you may discover some things about your business that will be uncomfortable.

Listen and Talk

Listen to, and answer, customers' phone calls. Respond to customers' letters and e-mails. Just a few hours every month or two will add hugely to your understanding of what life is really like for your customers when they have to deal with your company.

Talk to Front-Line Staff

While you are listening to customers, take the time to talk to the people who do this job every day. You will be astounded not only by how much they know about your customers, but also by how many ideas they have to improve the quality of the customer's buying or service experience.

Visit Customers

Visit your customers, but don't turn it into a royal procession. Do it at short, or better still no, notice. Don't allow your people to manipulate who you see or what you discuss – just turn up and see what happens!

Meet the Influencers

If you sell to businesses, don't only meet your opposite number in the largest accounts. Meet with users, buyers and financial decision makers, in fact anyone who influences the sale, from a cross-section of customers who are new and old, large and small, happy and disgruntled. Use the opportunity to understand their perceptions of the buying process and the relative merits of your company.

Act Like a Customer

Telephone your company (or get a friend to do it for you), perhaps with a valid complaint worthy of your attention. You may be amazed by just how difficult your staff are to talk to. You might also be horrified by the quality of the response.

Read Customer Correspondence

Ask to see a sample of customer correspondence regularly, both good and bad. Read not just what customers say, but how they say it. Note the language they use – and contrast it with the language your company uses in response. Handle one of the customer complaints that normally gets picked up by your secretary or assistant; it's good for your soul, if not your blood pressure.

Attend Customer Research

Sit in on some customer research. Observe focus group discussions, but resist the urge to intervene. At one customer research session, where the participants were discussing the merits of a series of advertising treatments, a senior manager viewing the proceedings became so incensed that the customers were missing the point, he burst in to put them straight!

Hear It From the Horse's Mouth

Insist that all research commissioned by your company is presented without any intervention by the marketing or research department. Let the people who have completed the research present their findings directly. If you don't like what you hear (unless the methodology or execution is flawed), take time to understand why the findings are as they are. Resist the temptation to shoot the messenger, or to pursue more research until you achieve results that support your prejudices. If they do not exist already, introduce research programmes designed to understand why customers defect and why you fail to win their business. If possible, include your competitors' customers in your sample.

Instigate Mystery Shopping

Initiate a structured mystery shopping programme to help provide some idea of scale for the issues you have identified. Include as many senior managers as possible. If they live the experience and understand what it is really like to be a customer, it is far more likely that they will also become advocates and supporters of lasting change.

Spread the Gospel

Above all, get as many colleagues as possible to understand how valuable it can be to the company if they make just a little time to pay attention to customers. Even if it has to be done by coercion, that is better than nothing. It is far preferable, however, to win the argument and encourage them to act in this way because it will help them do their jobs better and, as a result, create greater shareholder value.

None of these activities will, of itself, increase customer value. They will all nevertheless improve the quality of your understanding of who your customers are, what and how they think, and what place your firm has to play in their lives and businesses.

This understanding of customers is, of course, only a means to an end. It is merely one part of the jigsaw that allows a customer-focused business to take decisions that will maximize the long-term value of the organization. This individual jigsaw piece has to be placed in the right space within the puzzle and that requires a context – a view of the entire picture. That context is your company's business strategy: a strategy that must recognize the competitive, market, economic and political environments within which your company operates, but is informed by your insight into customers.

Chapter 3

Look Before You Leap
Developing a Customer-focused Strategy

'Would you tell me, please, which way I ought to go from here?'
'That depends a good deal on where you want to get to,' said the Cat.
'I don't much care where,' said Alice.
'Then it doesn't matter which way you go,' said the Cat.
Alice's Adventures in Wonderland, Lewis Carroll

A leading UK service company decided that it needed to diversify its business portfolio, so it commissioned a well-known firm of international strategy consultants to help it identify what it should do, and how. The consultants approached the task professionally and thoroughly, using the company's competencies as the building blocks for appraising the various ideas that arose.

The project proceeded well and a new concept surfaced comparatively quickly that was complementary to the core business. It reflected the company's heritage; built on its worldwide customer and operational reach; and capitalized on its experience at managing mass consumer markets. It was also less seasonal and, by working through third-party business partners, the company believed that it could achieve critical mass quickly and affordably.

The Board approved the business plan, new managers were hired and the building of the necessary infrastructure began. The initial reaction from potential customers appeared to be lukewarm, but this was put down to the fact that it was an innovative concept that would take some time to become recognized and appreciated by the market. The company ploughed on, sinking many millions of pounds into the project, and launched on its planned date.

Key prospects could now view and touch the facility, as well as seeing it demonstrated live. They were impressed, but still reluctant. The company now needed customers urgently and, in order to achieve some income, concluded a variety of deals with brand-leading partners who would provide the new organization with momentum and credibility.

Unfortunately, the expected new custom did not flow in as expected. Business growth targets were consistently missed and the Board was beginning to question the wisdom of its investment. To cap it all, one of the inaugural customers, the leading company in its sector, decided not to renew its annual contract. The situation looked dire, and the company considered closure and write-off. The managing director of the parent company was loath to pursue this option, however. In his heart, he believed that the business concept was still sound, but that the customer strategy was weak. Perhaps there could be other ways of approaching the market that would be more successful?

Another team of specialist market and customer-management consultants was hired to identify the problems and explore the options. This second group studied the business model; talked to customers and prospects; identified new service concepts and ways of reaching and serving the market; and modelled and appraised the outcomes for their potential business success. Would it be possible to turn the business around, would it have to be closed, or could it be sold off in a fire sale?

In-depth investigation indicated that the business itself was actually quite sound. It had an excellent product and the service levels were high. There was evidence of market demand and environmental factors looked favourable. However, the losses that it had incurred rendered it unsaleable at a worthwhile price. Closure would also have been extremely expensive and would have harmed the parent company's brand. It was decided to focus on the company's trading strategy and give the new business one last chance.

The team concentrated on the company's customers and prospects. Why had partners been reluctant to sign? Why had their contracts lapsed? How could the company reconfigure itself in order to have a more attractive customer proposition, while moving itself towards profitability? A range of options were identified and modelled. Many were discarded, but a few appeared to be possibilities that could not be ignored. Those with potential were tried out by small task forces within the business, who were given specific targets and deadlines. The board needed a result swiftly.

Very quickly, it became apparent that a number of the options were going to be successful. Why? Because they started with the customer as the focus and then, when the proposition could be proven to satisfy customer needs, the company asked itself what it needed to do differently in order to trade profitably under the new model. The previous management had simply fallen in love with the business's operational capabilities, believing that the service would then 'sell itself'.

Unfortunately, life is not like that. The good news was that the development and implementation of customer-focused strategies reversed the fortunes of the new business. The whole company, including the previously loss-making subsidiary, was sold some time later for over £800 million.

WHAT IS CUSTOMER-FOCUSED STRATEGY?

'Action this day,' exhorted Winston Churchill. The action-oriented business manager has been lauded ever since. However, action without objectives will consist of, at best, a random set of loosely inter-connected tasks that may, but more likely will not, achieve any sustainable improvement in business performance.

Objectives without a strategy will lack the vision, direction and certainty to galvanize any organization to pursue a common goal.

Ambiguity between the chosen strategy and the tactics designed to realize it will simply fail to achieve any improvement in long-term shareholder value. Change may occur, but it will probably be short-term, irrelevant to customers and inconsequential to both shareholders and other stakeholders alike. Resist the urge to take action until you have developed and tested a strategy designed to realize true customer focus. Yet this essential step is one with which many companies struggle and is probably the primary reason that so few organizations have seen any significant and lasting value from their customer-management initiatives.

Strategy Defined

If the rhetoric and gobbledegook are stripped away, a customer or market strategy can be simply defined as 'a plan designed to achieve corporate objectives by securing competitive advantage'. In the customer-focused organization, many of these objectives will relate to the markets within which the company wishes to compete, the customers it wishes to serve and, of course, the ways in which it will profit from these important choices. The strategy will involve having clearly articulated, affordable and achievable goals, and it will specify a clear path towards their realization. Once the direction has been selected, the task then becomes to do things better, faster or more cheaply than competitors. But without a clear direction, any path is as good as any other, organizational focus is lost, customers and staff become confused, and corporate anarchy and infighting are likely to ensue.

Setting strategy is therefore about making choices and selecting paths. Consider what can occur if the essential analyses and decisions are not made intelligently and communicated persuasively.

The Need for Vision

The organization will have no vision. It will probably have a clear set of financial goals, but significantly less clarity about how such objectives will be achieved by serving markets and customers – the essential *and only* drivers of revenues and profits. Without an overriding vision, all strategies will be 'good' strategies and there will be no way in which they can be appraised for their ability to achieve corporate goals – or whether they will simply add an unbearable burden of additional cost.

Strategic Consistency

There will be no clear and unambiguous specification of the markets and customers to be served. Products and services will be selected opportunistically, with little or no recognition of the competitive environment in which they will be launched, or whether they are building the required brand values and levels of long-term customer profitability. All customers will be 'good' customers, regardless of their characteristics and behaviour. Customer service will be considered as 'good', because it makes for happier customers; or 'bad', because it adds to cost and depresses short-term profitability.

Customer Profitability

Even if – through accident, historical precedent or a sheer lack of management creativity – the market and customer choices have been made, it may be far from clear which customers are profitable and which destroy value. It will be extremely unlikely that the characteristics of those customers with the greatest current or potential value will have been identified. Without such measures, it will be impossible to decide how much the organization can justify spending to acquire, retain and service each group.

Staff Commitment

There will be no staff commitment or initiative and meaningful innovation will occur by chance alone. Competent people will be reluctant to join, or support, an organization that lacks ambition or direction. Initiative will be stifled because nobody will be aware of what it is they can do to make a difference; and new ideas will lack the essential focus on customer needs and the key competitive issues.

Cost Control

There will be an over-emphasis on cost control, with less consideration of revenues and their sources. Conversely, there may well be over-investment in technology, believing it to be a panacea, with no coherent view about how it will be employed to acquire and keep more of the right customers, or to make existing customers more profitable.

Confusion and Alienation

Finally, there will be no alignment between the objectives of the organization and the tactics that it selects to achieve them. Action plans will comprise a disparate set of 'good ideas', which individually might seem attractive or appropriate but collectively send contradictory messages that confuse and alienate staff, customers, prospects and suppliers alike.

If strategic analysis and direction in the management of markets and customers are so important, why do so many companies find it difficult, or even impossible, to translate their financial objectives and corporate goals into profitable market or customer strategies and plans? Because it can be complicated and time-consuming! Consider just some of the current issues with which strategists in most industries worldwide must wrestle.

STRATEGY IN CONTEXT

Markets are becoming more global and the cultural differences that separated them, and provided each with a unique character and set of issues, are disappearing. National markets are becoming more homogeneous, which can simplify the planning task but also raises a whole new set of challenges related to building, sustaining and delivering global brands. Never has there been a greater need to ensure consistency in terms of product quality, service standards and distribution. Concurrently, technology is enabling the development of new media, which are inexorably contributing towards the fragmentation of established markets and communications channels; and increasing the costs of reaching, and servicing, both customers and prospects.

A Commoditized World

Competition has never been greater. Technology, transport and infrastructure developments, combined with the worldwide growth in the service economy, have all made it easier, faster and cheaper for companies to enter new markets – especially those that have yet to face the full force of competition. This, in turn, is increasing the pace of commoditization, placing even greater pressure on prices and margins and making meaningful and sustainable differentiation harder than ever to achieve.

Consumer Sophistication

Consumers are becoming more sophisticated and, because they are more knowledgeable, they are increasingly shopping around for the best deals, often using new media such as the Internet to compare and contrast products, prices and propositions. Not only is this further reinforcing the downward pressure on prices and margins, it is also resulting in greater customer promiscuity, especially among those who are aware of their relative value and attraction. This increasing consumer sophistication, combined with lower levels of customer loyalty and the failure of 'loyalty marketing', is inexorably leading towards a need for greater levels of investment in customer acquisition, retention and service, which in turn further squeeze profitability through added cost and the need for greater product and service personalization.

Consumer Expectations

Expectations are rising. Consumers are becoming more and more irritated by the tools and technologies – the Internet and automated telephone handling systems to name just two – that make matters easier and cheaper for the organization, but mean that *they* have to do all the work. Consumers with the greatest value, especially in business-to-business markets, are increasingly expecting some of the savings to be passed back by way of lower prices, discounts or added value.

Added Costs

The newer, electronic media are also adding to costs, rather than increasing customer satisfaction and reducing overheads. Not only are people using e-mail 'because they can', but they expect an immediate response from what they see as an immediate medium. First Direct, the UK's first telephone-based banking service, noticed a sustained increase in call volumes, and costs, in comparison with its traditional HSBC branch network model, simply because it had made customer contact so easy and convenient. Egg, an Internet bank, was astonished by the volume of e-mails that it received following its launch.

Legacy Income Streams

This need for greater customer focus goes hand in hand with the need for many organizations, particularly those with institutional shareholders, to protect and grow their established income streams. The conflicting challenges of adopting new practices while simultaneously improving revenues and profits consistently are indeed hard to balance. This fear of jeopardizing historical income flows can also result in organizational chaos.

Those companies that have attempted greater customer focus have often redesigned their structures around customer segments or groups, rather than products, which is the more established route. However, the migration path from product to customer orientation is far from straightforward, leaving many companies in transition limbo, with a matrix organization within which responsibilities and accountabilities, for both customer management and profitability, are far from clear.

Fear of Change

When all these macro developments are combined with the natural human fear of change, and the resistance that it engenders among management and staff alike, the task of the customer and market strategist has never been more complicated, difficult and time consuming. However, the forces that make the task so complex are the very same forces that render the development of an appropriate, affordable, practical *and profitable* strategy for managing customers and markets so essential. So what are the steps?

DEVELOPING CUSTOMER-FOCUSED STRATEGY

Many models of the strategy-development process have been designed throughout the years. Most will look similar to Figure 3.1.

It is not the purpose of this book to discuss the relative merits of the various, and numerous, strategic planning methodologies and models. Each organization, or planner, will find or develop a structure that suits its needs and the challenges that it faces. There certainly is no 'right' or 'wrong' method – just those that work and those that don't. However, it is worth taking some time to discuss the essential ingredients, whatever the model used.

Vision and Objectives: a Customer Perspective

The process must start with a vision for the way in which the organization wishes to manage its customers, and the high-level objec-

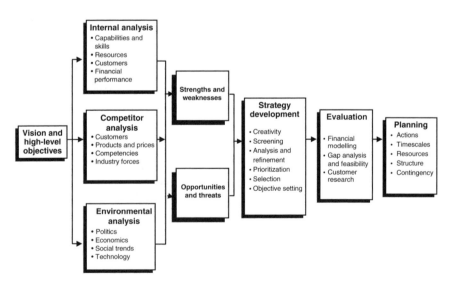

Figure 3.1   Strategy formulation
Reproduced by permission of Valoris Ltd

tives to which it aspires. Without a customer-focused vision, it will be impossible to place any parameters around the task and the planning process will be stifled at birth, or drowned under an unmanageable plethora of alternatives. The available options and, therefore, the number and scope of analyses required will be so large that progress will be extremely slow – or even impossible.

The vision should clearly state what the organization is seeking to achieve. One simple and straightforward method is to describe what the customer's experience will be like when the vision has been achieved. If you put yourself in the customer's shoes, it is significantly easier to describe the outcome and the experience.

The vision must, simultaneously, be supported by a set of high-level objectives. These are most likely to be financial, although if there are some 'givens' they should be made explicit at this stage. For example, an insurance company may specify that its revenues will come exclusively from the sale of insurance products; or that all products will be sold under a single, common brand; or that only a particular customer group will be served. While this might sound limiting, it is better to be specific about any constraints at the outset. Such clarity will avoid a company such as Axa diversifying into other, perhaps unrelated, businesses outside its core competences; or American Express undermining its carefully crafted brand; or Coutts becoming a mass-market bank, when to do so might fundamentally compromise the positioning and commercial future of the business as a whole.

Setting the vision and high-level objectives is the responsibility of the chief executive and/or the Board, in conjunction with the planner. Only in this way will the market and customer strategies and plans that follow be aligned with those of all other parts of the organization, and be sufficient to meet, or exceed, shareholder and stakeholder requirements.

The Need for Strategic Analysis

The next step comprises analysis, which may or may not be concurrent with the strategy-development phase. It might seem odd to recommend that strategy might be postulated simultaneously with analysis, or even before it is complete, but the process does not have to be linear. In fact, some of the most creative ideas are not born from rigorous analysis but from off-the-wall thinking, with the subsequent analysis designed to prove, or disprove, the creative hypothesis.

For example, Barclaycard was not launched in response to an identifiable consumer demand, as credit cards were new to the UK in 1966. The Switch debit card was not conceived by meticulous planners, but by entrepreneurs within NatWest, the Royal Bank of Scotland and the (then) Midland Bank who were attempting to rescue a significant (and failed) investment in EftPos UK, which was made, in turn, to reduce their cheque transaction-processing costs.

The analysis phase typically consists of three parts: internal, competitive and environmental. Let's consider each in turn.

Identifying Capabilities and Resources

Internal analysis is, by definition, introspective. Who are the customers currently being served? What do they look like? What are their attitudes, needs and preferences? From which other companies do they buy and why? What share of the customer's wallet does the company have? How profitable are the customers or customer segments? Which products or services are most profitable and why? How frequently do customers buy? How long do they stay? What do they cost to service? Which distribution channels are most cost-effective?

The list is long and should be as exhaustive as is practical. The key is to build a complete picture of existing customers and markets in order to build on *strengths* and, hopefully, eradicate *weaknesses* with the ensuing strategies.

Developing Competitive Insight

Who are the company's competitors? What strategies are they pursuing? What market share does each hold? Are they growing or declining, and why? Are they more, or less, profitable and what are the drivers of their financial performance? Which customers, or customer groups, are they serving? What products do they sell and at what price points? What do their customers think of them – and of your company? What makes each competitor different to, or better than, your business? What are the competitive forces acting on all the players in the market? How might they react to your new initiatives?

Again, there are no right and wrong ways of addressing these questions, the key is simply to develop an in-depth understanding of customer and market dynamics, the assumptions that each of your competitors holds about the market, the strategies they are pursuing and their absolute and relative performance.

There are a wide variety of analytical tools open to the customer strategist. All have their strengths and weaknesses in attempting to order and make sense of the wealth of competitor data that you are, or should be, collecting. Michael Porter's model of generic competitive strategy is just one, but is a useful starting point for plotting the ways in which each competitor is addressing the market.

Are competitors seeking to differentiate themselves? Is one or more attempting to drive down cost so that it might become, or remain, the industry cost leader? Or are they focusing on particular product groups or customer segments and striving to be different, or the lowest-cost supplier, in their chosen area of focus?

Porter's Five Forces analysis can also be helpful in providing insight into both current and potential competitive threats. Most

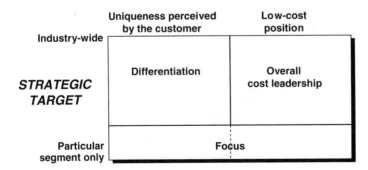

Figure 3.2 Generic competitive strategies
Reproduced from *Competitive Strategy* by Michael Porter with permission of
The Free Press

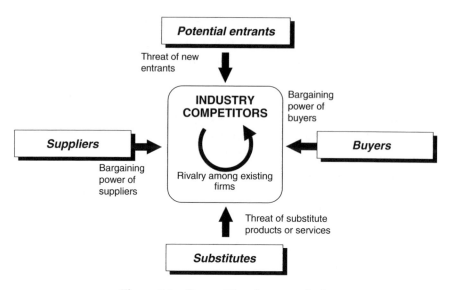

Figure 3.3   Competitive forces analysis
Reproduced from *Competitive Strategy* by Michael Porter with permission of
The Free Press

competitor analyses address existing rivals only. Porter takes it
further by considering new entrants and substitutes, by recognizing the crucial bargaining power of both suppliers and buyers – and
the critical importance of both in setting an appropriate competitive
strategy.

APPRAISING THE WORLD OUTSIDE

The strategist must consider the environment in which the organization trades. One simple and widely used tool is PEST analysis of
political, economic, societal and technological factors. Are there
any *political* or legal developments under consideration or review
that might change the nature of the competitive threat? For
instance, the abolition of the Net Book Agreement, concerning
resale price maintenance in the retail bookselling industry, had a
profound impact on industry dynamics. Increasing regulation in
the financial services industry is adding considerably to the cost
and complexity of product design and operations.

Which *economic* changes, or forecasts, might influence consumer demand or the margins achievable? Is the economy heading for recession? Is unemployment rising? What is likely to happen to interest rates and house prices? How is consumer confidence changing? Are levels of corporate taxation due to increase? Which segments of the population will be hit the hardest and what is the likely level of organizational exposure?

How do *societal* changes affect consumer behaviour or cost structures? Will Internet usage ever become as popular as the telephone and, if so, when and what will it mean for price competition and operational cost structures? Will customer promiscuity further fragment markets and increase the costs of customer acquisition and retention for all? Will consumer sophistication accelerate the pace of commoditization and render differentiation an increasingly difficult strategic path to follow?

Will there be a backlash against the deployment of *technologies* that depersonalize the already fragile relationships between commercial organizations and their customers? Conversely, what new technologies are available, or under development, that might revolutionize industry cost structures or facilitate improved service levels, for example?

A thorough understanding of competitive threats, combined with a detailed environmental appraisal, enables the strategist to identify the *opportunities* and *threats* that might be capitalized on or must be countered. The analytical phase involves collection, collation and distillation until the key market- and customer-related issues have been identified with rigour and certainty.

The Criticality of Creativity

Developing a commercially successful customer-focused strategy is both a science and an art. It is a science, in as much as it should be built on rigorous analysis and the intelligent distillation of all relevant data, using tools and techniques that enable complex relationships to be readily understood. It is an art, because very few analytically based strategies have delivered the creative breakthroughs that have revolutionized industry dynamics – and the personal fortunes of the entrepreneurs who have led the charge. Strategy by analysis can, if not leavened by creative thinking, lead to the reinforcement of established wisdom and creeping incrementalism: more of the same, but slightly different each year. Creativity, on the other hand, must be constrained by rational thought and analysis. Think the unthinkable, but only bet the mortgage when the numbers have been run!

It is for these reasons that the strategy can be developed concurrently with the analysis, if it is managed so that neither predominates. Indeed, it can sometimes be advantageous to do so, using different people with different thinking skills and experience, in order to avoid constraining the blue-sky visionaries or stifling the insightful analysts. Both steps are essential and each organization must find a method that suits its style, as well as the competitive environment in which it is placed.

As has been said, developing strategy is about making choices; and the customer-focused organization begins its strategic thinking with consideration of the drivers of revenues and profits.

The Profit Hierarchy

The goal of any strategy should be to increase long-term profits and the return to shareholders. However, despite the seeming multiplicity of options, there are in fact relatively few levers that can be pulled, as Figure 3.4 demonstrates.

Increased profit arises from either a greater volume of product or service sales, or enhanced margins. Volume is a function of market expansion that, in turn, arises from either serving new markets or new customer groups. Igor Ansoff rather neatly encapsulated the choices in his eponymous matrix, which also ascribed a level of risk to each potential strategy, from low-risk *business development*, involving the more efficient sale of existing products to existing customers, through to high-risk *diversification*, or the development of new products for customers currently not served by the company.

Volume-related income can also arise from increasing market share, which can only come from either persuading existing customers to spend more, or acquiring new ones. Margin improve-

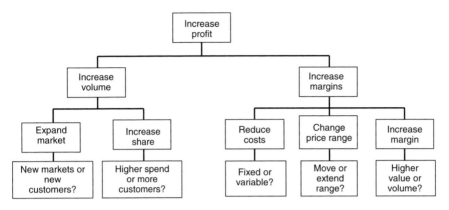

Figure 3.4 The profit hierarchy
Reproduced by permission of Valoris Ltd

PRODUCTS

	Existing	New
Existing	**1** Business development	**2** Product development
MARKETS/ CUSTOMERS		
New	**3** Market development	**4** Diversification

Figure 3.5 The Ansoff matrix
Reproduced from *The New Corporate Strategy* by Igor Ansoff by permission of
John Wiley & Sons

ments, on the other hand, can be driven by reduced fixed or variable costs, price enhancements or economies of scale.

Compatibility with Corporate Strategy

The selection of the most appropriate market and customer strategy must, of course, be driven by the competitive strategy of the organization as a whole. There must be convergence between the over-arching corporate strategy and the ways in which customers and markets are managed. Any weakness, or incompatibility, in the link between the two will undermine the organization's positioning and credibility and affect its chances of success, probably fatally. If what an organization says about itself publicly is contradicted at the point of sale by staff who have been given, or believe, different messages, customers will become confused and disillusioned. For example, the Midland Bank advertised itself as 'The Listening Bank' when its retail banking staff listened no more or less than those of its competitors. British Rail famously stated 'We're getting there', but the resulting customer backlash resulted in a quick and embarrassing withdrawal.

So let's consider the requirements of and implications for the customer-focused organization of each of the three 'generic' strategy alternatives espoused by Michael Porter.

SEEKING TO BE DIFFERENT

A company seeking to be different will need to look for ways in which it can add value for its customers. Such value may relate to the product itself, in terms of its physical features, design or brand values; the ways in which the product is distributed; or the level or nature of service provided, either pre- or post-sale.

Guinness, for example, is differentiated from its rivals not only by its unique look and taste, but also by its distinctive and memorable advertising. Bang & Olufsen's electrical products are famous for their design values. Internet-based bookseller Amazon offers an exceptional breadth of choice backed by high-speed delivery and some sophisticated cross-sales software that recommends further products based on past purchases. Dell is renowned for its attention to customer service.

Nevertheless, differentiation usually adds to cost and complexity, and brings four further challenges.

Targeting

Targeting is critical. If the investment in adding value through differentiation is not to be wasted, it is imperative that the product is targeted efficiently and cost-effectively at those prospects and customers who will appreciate its differences and will therefore value it sufficiently to pay a price premium.

Meaningful

It is essential that the sources of differentiation are meaningful for the customers selected. Unless the differences are valued, they are hardly likely to pay for them – certainly not more than once.

Profit Relationship

There has to be a clear relationship between the benefits offered and their cost, and increased corporate revenues and profits. Without such a relationship, it is likely that any attempts at differentiation will simply erode margins.

Product, Service or Both?

There also has to be agreement on whether competitive advantage will be achieved by differentiating the product itself, the service that supports it, or both (see Figure 3.6).

Systemic Differentiation

Systemic differentiation provides the greatest source of competitive advantage, but is the hardest and typically the most expensive to

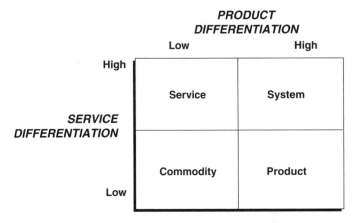

Figure 3.6 The differentiation matrix
Reproduced by permission of Valoris Ltd

achieve and sustain. As an example, Kuoni has been voted 'long-haul tour operator of the year' by UK travel agents for the last 19 years. It combines a high-quality product with admirable service standards, in an industry not renowned for its customer focus. For these reasons, the company can command a price premium that sustains its business model when all around it are discounting as the norm.

Product Differentiation

Swatch is a fine example of product differentiation. The Swiss watchmakers were being taken apart by their Far Eastern competitors, who had achieved the same product reliability at a fraction of the price. Swatch's response involved developing a range of relatively cheap-to-produce, fashion-led products that were not only of very original design, but also (and here was the stroke of genius) of limited availability. The market demand was such that the company was able to price its products disproportionately to their cost and reap the profits accordingly.

Service Differentiation

First Direct is regarded as probably one of the greatest examples of service differentiation. It is open 365 days a year, 24 hours a day. Banking representatives answer the phone quickly and whoever you talk to can effect the required transaction equally efficiently. It offers competitive pricing, interest rates and product features, although the latter are not too dissimilar to those of competitors. And perhaps most importantly, its staff appear to value their customers – and communicate accordingly. Not surprisingly, First Direct is reported to have the most loyal and satisfied customers of any bank in the UK today.

Similarly, hi-fi retailer Richer Sounds is acknowledged as providing far higher levels of customer service than its rivals, yet its products are far from unique. It observed, quite sensibly, that it had no control over its manufacturing suppliers in terms of product design or innovation. It also identified that the levels of product knowledge among its competitors were desultory and that there was therefore a significant advantage to be gained from making its sales staff more professional, friendly and knowledgeable.

In contrast, many of the gas, electricity, water and telephone utilities are completely undifferentiated from one another in terms of either their product or their service offerings, which may be, of course, why they are experiencing such intense price pressure, escalating levels of customer disaffection and attrition.

LEADING ON COST

Cost leadership can be an equally effective strategy, but also has some important implications for the customer-management strategist. While stripping out cost and either passing the savings on by way of lower prices or making above-average returns would seem sensible, there are some key principles.

Understanding What Customers Value

It is essential to understand what it is that customers actually value (which may or may not be what they tell you, or what management believes) so that essential features of the customer proposition are not eradicated. In the personal savings market, for example, it is tempting to believe that all customers are rational and that the interest rate offered will be the prime determinant of competitive success. This is simply not true in practice, as a large proportion of savers are attracted by other factors such as the ease and convenience of access to their money; or because they already have an established relationship; or because the savings institution was recommended to them by friends or family. The key is knowing what the prospects and customers your company seeks to serve want and, most importantly, are prepared to change suppliers to secure.

The mission of one European TV channel, covering over 80 million households in 15 languages, was to offer consumers the greatest variety of programmes. However, its customers also included distributors (cable and satellite system operators) and advertisers. Managers in the business believed price to be key, but subsequent analysis indicated that distributors particularly valued their relationships, while subscribers were more interested in the product itself.

These findings changed the nature of the interaction between the company and its key customer groups. A strategy was designed for distributors based on customer value, rather than geographic boundaries; while the offering to subscribers was tailored to meet the needs of key customer segments based on the identified value of each.

Applying the Advantage

Airline easyJet unashamedly trades on its low-cost position, with all elements of its customer proposition and service-delivery system aligned behind this strategy. These include Internet-based booking systems, pricing that increases as the departure date nears, ticketless check-in, paid-for in-flight refreshments and a boarding policy that will not compromise departure punctuality for late customer arrivals, regardless of how upset, or important, the customer is. In a world market littered with airline failures, easyJet has continued to grow in both passenger numbers and profits.

Trailfinders is another company that built its initial success through cost leadership. It sells air tickets, primarily consisting of an airline's unsold inventory, at discounted prices. The margins were slim, but its overheads were significantly below those of its competitors – and its service levels were exemplary. Unsurprisingly, customer loyalty was very high – and a significant proportion of its business growth came from repeat purchase and personal recommendation.

FOCUSING ON MARKETS OR CUSTOMERS

Focus, the last of Porter's three alternatives, has two possible components. Their common element is the requirement to concentrate effort and resources on particular markets or customer groups. However, thereafter the opportunity is a choice between differentiating your company's products or services to better meet the needs of the selected target audience(s); or providing the lowest-cost alternative for a potentially attractive segment perhaps previously ignored, or disadvantaged, by competitors. For this strategic path, somewhat similar customer-management issues arise.

The Importance of Customer Value

Most important is the need to identify accurately the specific areas of focus. Not only must the chosen markets or segments be substantial, homogeneous in their requirements, comparatively stable (as far as possible) and accessible, they must also be likely to yield the return required to justify the investment and risk. While it seems obvious, this last criterion is the one most frequently ignored or glossed over, because it requires understanding and modelling likely financial returns. Such modelling necessitates a calculation of potential customer value, which in turn demands a level of insight into customer profitability that is frequently lacking.

The Need for Knowledge

Similarly, focusing on particular markets and customers requires in-depth understanding of the chosen audience's needs, attitudes and supplier-switching behaviour. Focus implies greater knowledge and a more specialized product or service proposition that meets market requirements more accurately, or at lower cost, than do competitors. Arguably easier to achieve than mass-market strategies, focus demands greater insight into niche customer motivations, a far more in-depth understanding of competitors and a business model that is not dependent on achieving high sales volumes.

Cost vs Differentiation

Lastly, the organization needs to balance, or select between, the achievement of comparative cost advantage and the realization of differentiation (see Figure 3.7). Without some form of cost advantage, at best competitors will find it easy to copy and negate the initiative; while at worst the business will be pursuing a path that

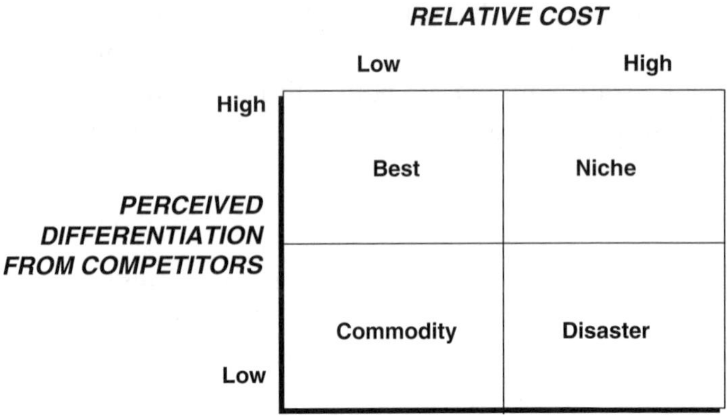

RELATIVE COST

	Low	High
High	Best	Niche
Low	Commodity	Disaster

PERCEIVED DIFFERENTIATION FROM COMPETITORS

Figure 3.7 The cost/differentiation matrix
Reproduced by permission of Valoris Ltd

is simply unaffordable and unsustainable. Without meaningful differentiation, the market niche will also quickly be exploited by competitors who may not previously have spotted the opportunity, but will not be slow to copy and catch up.

Direct Line, the UK's first direct insurer, focused on a particular market sector when it launched and by doing so achieved significant cost leadership. The company only insured careful drivers, in certain areas and between certain ages. It offered a direct telephone service that minimized its investment in premises and staff. It was thus able to offer lower prices and, by using what was at the time sophisticated customer-management technology, provided a level of service that engendered higher levels of loyalty and profitability than its competitors. This also allowed Direct Line to operate with little or no competitor response for several years during which it built a significant market share – an appropriate reminder of the critical need for competitor analysis.

Agreeing how the organization will, or should, compete is only the starting point for the development of a customer strategy. It provides the essential framework for the company and, if adequately and persuasively communicated, the 'glue' ensuring that all parts of the company pull in the same direction. However, it does not define what should be done to manage each customer, or customer segment, on a day-to-day basis.

THE CUSTOMER LIFECYCLE

Traditionally, managers have approached this task by considering the lifecycle of the typical customer, breaking the challenge down according to the customer's status and the contribution to sales that each makes at the different stages in the purchasing lifetime (see Figure 3.8).

The Five Stages of Lifecycle Management

Initially, of course, customers cost money to acquire and welcome. Thereafter, it is to be expected that sales will grow as they become more familiar with the company, its products, services and *modus operandi*. The task at this second stage is, therefore, to cross-sell other products within the portfolio, or to up-sell by encouraging a greater frequency, volume or value of purchases by the newly acquired customer.

As familiarity further increases and customer sales grow, the challenge turns to maximizing the return on the initial acquisition investment. However, few customers last forever, and typically sales will either cease or begin to fall as alternative suppliers are

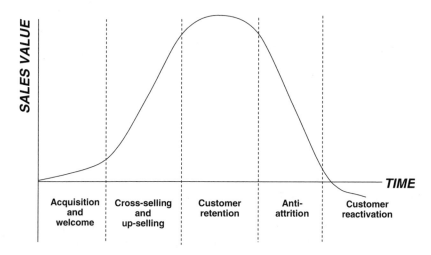

Figure 3.8 The customer lifecycle
Reproduced by permission of Valoris Ltd

sought or customers are lured away by more attractive and competitive product offerings. It is at this time that organizations seek to put in place measures designed to retain as many customers as possible, often by adding value to the customer proposition or by offering purchase volume or value discounts, for example.

Finally, the company loses the customer. Nevertheless, the seemingly astute manager recognizes that, because such customers have bought in the past, they may well have a higher predisposition to buy again than would a new, cold prospect. Consequently, investment is made in attempting to reactivate them so as to recreate their previous buying behaviour.

At first blush, such a model looks extremely logical and efficient. It concentrates effort and resources on customers according to the specific challenges relating to each as they pass through their 'natural' buying cycle. However, *if not combined with customer-value analysis*, the lifecycle model can have serious flaws and be responsible for massive amounts of wasted expenditure on inappropriate communications, thereby depressing corporate profitability. Just consider some of the implications.

The Need for Customer Orientation

The model is company, not customer, oriented. The goals at each stage relate to those of the organization, not the customer. It may be important for the company to increase its share of a customer's wallet through up-selling and cross-selling, for example, but this may not bear any relation to the customer and how he or she wishes to interact or purchase. For every new customer who becomes an immediate advocate and frequent buyer, there are many more who will purchase only once; or who will wish to buy at extended intervals; or who are simply not interested in any of the other products or services on offer by the company.

The Need for Personalized Objectives

The objectives, and often the communications that are employed to realize them, will be the same for each customer at each stage in their lifecycle, regardless of their needs. However, a customer who is new to buying via the telephone or the Net, for example, will have very different requirements to those of an experienced buyer who has been attracted from a competitor operating with a similar proposition. The former may require reassurance and a significant amount of information, while the latter may merely want the buying process to be made as easy and quick as possible.

The Need for Proactive Communications

Communications will be reactive and tactically driven by customer behaviour. The triggers for each customer communication or offer will probably be related to how the customer behaves, not necessarily what is in the best long-term commercial interests of the organization. So if purchase frequency declines or ceases, the customer may be regarded as potentially at risk, or lost, and anti-attrition or reactivation measures may be employed accordingly. While not all customers are equally profitable, the investment made by the company is frequently the same for all.

One international hotel chain ran a frequent-guest programme that required payment of an annual fee. In return, the customer received a range of benefits, such as late and express checkout and room upgrades. Amazingly, some consumers were paying their annual fee regularly, yet never staying at any of the hotels. Others were literally living in the hotels and spending tens of thousands of pounds each year. Despite these vast differences in value, each customer received the same communications, with the same offers, at the same frequency and at the same cost.

The Need for a Profit Focus

Customer lifecycle management will frequently focus on sales value, rather than contribution to profit or profit potential. Despite perhaps having similar historic sales values, there are often huge differences between the customer lifetime profitability and profit potential of specific individuals. Consider our hotel chain again. An international sales director, for whom travel is an integral part of the job, will be worth significantly more than a junior manager seconded to a regional office for a few months, despite their current sales values being the same. The leisure traveller who will only stay at weekends, when the room rate is discounted, will generate far lower levels of income in comparison with the mid-week guest paying the full rack rate.

The customer lifecycle model, if unrelated to customer value, will often result in margin being squandered. The frequent emphasis on adding value or discounting prices in order to retain, or reactivate, customers ignores the fact that there may be other, more important factors at play determining a customer's buying behaviour. Should a competitor have developed a more attractive or relevant proposition, lowering prices or adding inducements may simply increase the costs of servicing *all* customers, not simply those at risk of leaving.

The Need to Target Expenditure

Lastly, the model will tend to drive expenditure towards customer acquisition and reactivation in order to keep customer numbers as high as possible, despite the fact that such customers will usually be making significantly lower levels of contribution to corporate profitability. It is frequently the case that reactivated customers, while comparatively easy to reacquire, need escalating levels of inducement to purchase – and are significantly less loyal thereafter.

The board of one very large UK catalogue mail-order company measured its managing director on active customer numbers. Unsurprisingly, when volumes looked in danger, his customer managers simply spent more money on reactivation, despite empirical evidence that such activities were inherently unprofitable.

A different model is required, one that balances the commercial goals of the organization with the needs and characteristics of customers, or customer segments, their profitability and potential profitability. Only in this way can appropriate levels of investment be made in attracting and retaining the right customers with the right purchase behaviour patterns. If there is a real understanding of customers and their value, propositions, communications, operations and service levels can be designed that will maximize long-term customer profitability. Only by balancing the needs of the organization with the returns available from each customer, or segment, can true customer focus be achieved.

DECIDING AND EVALUATING ALTERNATIVES

Once the essential analyses of customer needs, characteristics and value have been made, the next step is to decide what do with each customer, or customer segment, in order to realize their latent value. The task is to develop and deliver attractive products at competitive prices to *profitable and potentially profitable* customers, seamlessly and consistently through whatever channels customers choose or prefer (and can be afforded), at the times when they want to buy. All of this must be supported by an appropriate brand, persuasive communications, affordable and appropriate levels of service support, and an advantageous generic competitive strategy. Simple!

Inspiration and Perspiration

It may be simple to say, but it is rather harder to do well.

There are no secrets to the process of developing a profitable customer-focused strategy. There is no magic formula. No analytical tool yet devised enables the strategist to input all the variables and be delivered a winning plan. As with most worthwhile activities, developing a customer-focused strategy involves both inspiration and perspiration. Inspiration is born from customer and market understanding; from the ability to understand industry and customer dynamics; and from the willingness to challenge established models and ways of doing things. Perspiration comes from being prepared rigorously to evaluate and screen each idea for its ability to balance corporate and customer needs; to re-analyse and refine market and customer data to sort the wheat from the chaff; and to prioritize ideas based on their ability to meet organizational objectives.

Screening Alternatives

Again, there is no 'correct' way to evaluate and prioritize customer-management strategy alternatives – there are only methods that work and those that do not. However, a variety of different models can be applied depending on relevance and circumstance. Balancing risk with expected revenue, as shown in Figure 3.9, is one method that forces a focus on commercial issues.

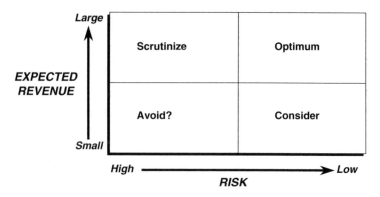

Figure 3.9   The risk/revenue matrix
Reproduced by permission of Valoris Ltd

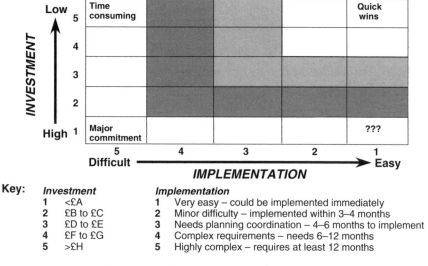

Key:

Investment		Implementation	
1	<£A	1	Very easy – could be implemented immediately
2	£B to £C	2	Minor difficulty – implemented within 3–4 months
3	£D to £E	3	Needs planning coordination – 4–6 months to implement
4	£F to £G	4	Complex requirements – needs 6–12 months
5	>£H	5	Highly complex – requires at least 12 months

Figure 3.10   Investment vs implementation
Reproduced by permission of Valoris Ltd

An equally valid alternative is to equate the investment required with the ease and speed of implementation (Figure 3.10). One significant advantage of this method is that it enables the identification of quick wins, as well as screening out those overly ambitious strategies that look attractive on paper, but would be impossible (for whatever reason) to implement cost-effectively.

Meeting Shareholder Needs

Creative thinking in customer-management strategy development must be balanced by a rigorous approach to appraisal. The customer-focused organization will of course be concerned with meeting customer needs, but will be equally exercised about whether shareholder value can be achieved. Will the proposed strategy deliver the sales and profits required, not merely in the short-term but over the long-term as well?

The Necessity for Iteration

Frequently, the initial answer to this question is 'no' and reiterations of initially appealing strategies are required if the financial forecast is to get close to corporate objectives and the strategic gap is to be closed (see Figure 3.11). It is at this stage that the insightful customer strategist revisits some of the earlier assumptions and decisions. Can productivity be improved by reducing costs, improving the sales mix, increasing prices, reducing discounts or improving sales force productivity, for example? Can market penetration be increased through share gains, or selling at higher values, or increasing purchase frequency? Will it be necessary to find, acquire and retain new customer groups, or expand into new

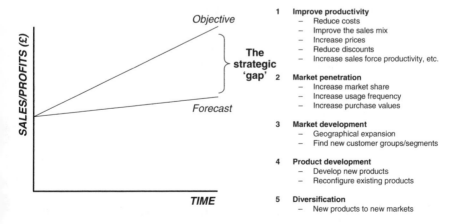

Figure 3.11   Gap analysis and strategy alternatives
Reproduced by permission of Valoris Ltd

territories, at home or abroad? Will new products be required, or can existing products be redesigned or reconfigured in order better to meet customer needs or counter competitive threats? Is a combination of some or all of these options required?

A word of warning: creating a plan that meets financial hurdle rates is easy. A small increase in revenues here, a modest reduction in costs there, and the required numbers can be forced out of the planning process. If those changes are fair and justified, this is all well and good. But if they are stretching the assumptions beyond realism into the realms of fantasy, the result will nearly always be disappointment, certainly for the investors and probably for the authors of the plan, who may find their career prospects severely limited.

Separating the Wheat From the Chaff

Financial modelling plays an important role in the strategy-appraisal process but to ensure customer focus it may be necessary to use customer or market research in order to understand more clearly the possible impacts of each of the strategy alternatives relating to attitudes and behaviour. While consumers are notoriously poor at accurately articulating their views and likely behaviours, especially in hypothetical contexts, research can be used to separate the obviously unattractive ideas from those that appear to make more sense to customers. Whatever the results, a healthy degree of scepticism and commercial common sense is required in interpreting and applying the results. History is littered with examples of great strategies and elegant plans that looked good in research, only to fail miserably when subsequently implemented.

ACTION PLANNING

The key in this final step is to ensure that whatever strategy is selected, the action plans are a true reflection of the chosen path. And it is at this stage that things frequently all go wrong.

Aligning Strategy and Tactics

While the need to align tactics with strategy seems obvious, the task is often not easy. On a superficial level, it might appear simple to identify, for example, that selling a new and truly differentiated product at rock-bottom prices is not commercially sensible. However, if a scale-sensitive market is dominated by a few key players with large market shares, volume sales may be needed to compete effectively, even if achievement of the necessary scale requires significant, and unprofitable, short-term expenditure. So what are some of the difficulties encountered at this last, critically important stage?

Vision

If you don't know where you are going, every path appears as good as any other. A common direction is therefore vital across the organization.

Single-mindedness

If, for example, focusing on particular customer groups or markets is the selected route, it is essential to be single-minded in pursuing this goal, regardless of whether there appears to be short-term advantage in adopting a more catholic approach.

Consistency

It is critical to ensure that the whole organization buys into and supports the strategy. Without understanding and commitment, even the best-laid plans will come to naught.

Knowledge

It is astonishing just how many organizations repeat the same mistakes year in and year out, through a lack of appropriate systems and procedures combined with natural levels of staff turnover. The best tactics are simply those that deliver the chosen strategy most effectively, whether that is at the lowest cost or in the highest volume. However, achieving tactical success is an iterative process that requires the recording of both successes *and* failures. The progressive organization celebrates failure rather than punishing it, but only if the initial premises were well conceived and the learning facilitates greater success in the future.

Performance Leverage

Customer focus entails aligning customer-management strategies and plans with commercial objectives. As such, the tactics employed should all be designed to address the key points of customer performance leverage in order to maximize the lifetime value of the customers acquired and, therefore, the organization's long-term profitability.

A successful customer-focused market and customer strategy balances corporate goals with the needs and profitability of customers. This is fine in principle, and an observation with which most senior managers would agree. However, despite the seemingly obvious nature of this assertion, very few organizations have achieved it. One of the key reasons for this failure is the inability to evaluate and quantify one half of the equation. Most businesses are extremely adept at measuring the achievement of internal, corporate goals through accounting systems that have been developed over many decades. The same is not true for measures of customer requirements, performance or value – and, after all, what gets measured gets managed. Measurement is therefore what we address in the next chapter.

Chapter 4

Measuring Your Way to Success
Allocating Resources for Maximum Effect

A strategy meeting is apt to generate more heat than light unless everybody is talking from a common set of numbers.

Up the Organization, Robert Townsend

For one of Europe's largest companies, trading in an industry that was rapidly consolidating, scale was becoming increasingly important. All its major competitors were on the acquisition trail. The firm decided that it, too, must grow and retained merchant bankers to identify appropriate targets. Soon a suitable company was short-listed, a medium-sized player based in the provinces. While it had a significant number of customers, the target company was under-performing compared to its larger rivals. Its brand was significantly less well known and its financial performance was lacklustre.

The acquiring organization made its approach, was greeted warmly and the laborious process of due diligence began. The accountants and bankers worked hard, nights and weekends included. This would be a multimillion-pound deal that could help transform the performance and competitiveness of both parties –

and add significantly to the fee incomes of the advisers. It all looked good. The investigations, largely financial, revealed nothing untoward and the deal was agreed and finalized. That was when it all started to go wrong.

Only when the acquiring company had actually moved its staff into the premises of its new subsidiary and the day-to-day process of integration had begun did the first alarm bells sound. While the subsidiary had a large and seemingly static customer base, it appeared to be spending a considerable amount of money each year on customer acquisition; in fact, far more than the industry average. During the due diligence process, it had been assumed that this was related to the weakness of the smaller company's brand and that association with the new, more illustrious parent would quickly rectify the problem.

In reality, the issue was far more deep seated. It appeared that customers were extremely transient and, because of this, the company had employed an ever-escalating range of incentives and price discounts to attract new business, the costs of which were largely hidden in the management accounts. Annual churn was high, and increasing, as the previous managers tried to keep the ship afloat by pumping more and more customers in at the front end of the business, while quickly losing them at the back through poor product design and inadequate servicing capabilities. Nobody had thought to attempt a calculation of the true value of the customers that were being acquired; only when the deal was done was it realized that the company had actually purchased a house of cards, which was about to fall over.

By contrast, another major organization bought a smaller rival, but this time the rival possessed a very strong brand of its own. It served the needs of a particular market segment, was trusted by its customers and they, in turn, appeared to be very loyal. It was true that the customers did not buy as frequently or at such high values as did those of the acquiring company, but the deal would bring massive economies of scale in terms of retail distribution and overheads could be streamlined to boost profitability.

Little did the acquirer know what a gem it was buying. Once the purchase was complete, the dynamics of the new customer base could be studied and contrasted with those of the parent company. The acquiring managers were rather more than pleasantly surprised to realize that the customers were not 'loyal' at all, they were inert. They were an unsophisticated bunch and simply did not shop around. They were also relatively price insensitive and were nervous about moving their custom.

The acquiring company had found, almost by chance, the perfect foil for its existing business, which comprised comparatively affluent, sophisticated and promiscuous customers. Once the excess costs of the merged businesses were purged, the new company established a pre-eminent position in its sector.

THE FAILURE OF MEASUREMENT

Question: How is the performance of most market- and customer-focused initiatives measured?

Answer: Inappropriately, inconsistently and in ways that reinforce poor commercial judgements and decisions.

The traditional, primarily accounting-based measures that are used to run businesses today are not only frequently irrelevant and inadequate for the management and development of customers, but can be positively misleading, often stimulating organizational behaviour that is completely counter to the creation of customer focus and long-term shareholder value.

Is this an overly harsh and unfair evaluation? We think not. As argued in previous chapters, customer focus is about balancing the requirements and needs of customers and prospects with the long-term corporate goals of the organization – and then aligning the business to deliver the chosen strategy seamlessly, consistently and profitably. One half of this equation is generally well served by financial and accounting teams; the other is woefully lacking any ongoing information that allows for insightful decision making and the measurement of performance. There are no prizes for guessing which statements apply to which aspect of customer focus! To prove the point, ask yourself whether your organization produces management information on the following three sets of questions with the same quality and regularity as it computes its profit and loss and balance sheet.

CUSTOMER ATTITUDE MEASURES

- What do customers think of your proposition, products, services, pricing and distribution capabilities?
- How do these perceptions differ from those held about your company by competitors' customers?
- What opinions do your customers have of your competitors' capabilities?
- Do their views differ by product group or customer segment?

The typical FTSE 100 company would struggle to answer these relatively straightforward, but critically important, questions in any form of structured and timely manner. Most smaller companies would find it impossible. It is true that a halfway competent and resourced marketing department could probably, given sufficient time, cobble something together that would appear credible. However, closer inspection would probably identify one or more of three critical issues.

Structured Tracking

First, there will probably be no mechanism in place to collect, analyse and report on these important customer views and perceptions in any structured and ongoing way that tracks absolute and relative competitive performance on a month-by-month basis. Should the information be collected at all, which is by no means universal, it will typically be through *ad hoc* studies that will be, at best, annual in their frequency; often a case of too little, too late.

Research and Analysis Comparability

Second, the information will rarely be capable of aggregation in a meaningful and consistent way. Product research will be conducted by different methods, and at different times, to pricing studies. The analysis of distribution capabilities will rarely be combined with or comparable to perceptions of customer service. For this reason, few organizations collect and report reliable, quantitative data on their customer proposition as a whole, simply compartmentalized aspects of it.

The Curse of Averaging

Third, the information will probably suffer from the curse of averaging. In order to achieve a valid data sample, and in the absence of more insightful guidance, the researcher will typically select a 'one-in-n' sample of the customer base, believing that it will provide a representative cross-section of views. Although of course it will, such sampling is meaningless. There can be no *single* set of customer perceptions. New customers will probably hold different views to those of more established shoppers. High-value customers will think differently to low-value testers. Multiple-product purchasers will probably feel more warmly towards the organization than will those customers who have bought only once. Retail customers may have very different characteristics to those who purchase via the telephone or the Net. To know that, for example, 60 per cent of customers perceive your company to offer 'value for money' is to potentially disguise (or worse, ignore) the fact that this figure will include some customers, or segments, where such satisfaction is 95 per cent – and some where it is 10 per cent.

CUSTOMER RETENTION MEASURES

- How do your current customer-retention rates compare with previous years and with those of your competitors?
- What are the triggers of customer defection – from, and to, your company?
- What types of customers are defecting and at what time?
- To which competitors are customers defecting, and why?
- How do the characteristics, behaviour and values of defecting customers contrast with those that remain?

Most companies will have some sort of measure of customer retention and defection. However, for many this will be crude and possibly misleading. One market-leading direct retailer simply calculated the number of active customers at the end of a year, added the new customers acquired during the subsequent year, and then subtracted the initial active customer base, expressing one as a percentage of the other. While it is laudable that any attempt at measurement was made, the chosen method of computation told the company nothing about who was defecting, the absolute or relative value of defectors, or why they were leaving.

Subsequent analysis indicated that the organization was very successful at acquiring new customers. It was also doing an excellent job of welcoming them and retaining their custom. A similar picture emerged for long-standing, high-value shoppers, on whom the company lavished significant resources. They were extremely satisfied and loyal. However, the business was haemorrhaging mid-value, but high-potential, customers with 2–5 years' shopping experience. As there was a proven and direct correlation between customer longevity and annual purchase value, this retailer was constraining its ability to grow customer and corporate profitability by masking the true nature of its customer-retention challenges.

Data Analysis and Knowledge

The issues facing this direct retailer were unusual and perhaps atypical, but they demonstrate how a lack of appropriate customer-data analysis and, hence, knowledge can have a profound impact on long-term profitability. More common is a lack of understanding about the behaviour of newly acquired customers, among whom, in almost every case, the greatest attrition occurs. In the membership organization illustrated in Figure 4.1, nearly 40 per cent of customers were being lost in the first year. However, this bald statistic masked the fact that there was a performance difference of approximately 20 per cent between the best- and worst-performing customer groups that, once the information was known, could be addressed by appropriate strategies for each.

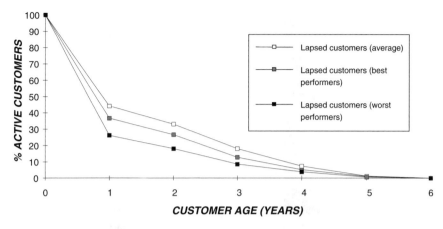

Figure 4.1 Attrition by customer life stage
Reproduced with permission of Valoris Ltd

Customer Migration

It has been proven time and again that different customers migrate for different reasons, and are therefore attracted by different competitors. In the credit-card industry, for example, a segmented analysis of NOPWorld Financial Research Survey (FRS) data clearly indicated that card issuers with a US heritage were attracting many new cardholders for reasons related to the price of the product; in this case, the annual interest rate charged (see Figure 4.2). However, further analysis of the reasons for card closure showed that these same issuers were not only losing many cardholders for exactly the same, price-related reason, but also significant proportions were switching to competitors in order to receive better card-usage incentives. Quite clearly, the different strategies required to retain these disparate customer groups must be designed, structured and targeted appropriately, or costly attrition will continue.

CUSTOMER VALUE MEASURES

- What are the current and potential lifetime values of your new and existing customers and how do they differ by customer or product segment?

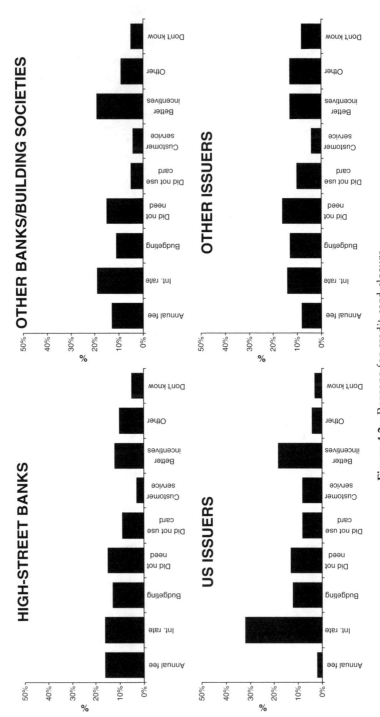

Figure 4.2　Reasons for credit-card closure
Reproduced with permission of NOP

- What percentage of your business volume and value does the top 20 per cent of customers represent?
- What is the difference in value creation between the top 10 per cent of customers and the bottom 10 per cent?
- What is the cost of replacing a lost customer compared to that of retaining an existing one?
- What would happen to profits if the retention rate increased by 5 per cent, 10 per cent etc.?

All these questions are perfectly reasonable, but of all the measures of customer performance, those related to customer value and profitability are the least likely to be known. There are two key reasons that even the most progressive and advanced organizations often shy away from even attempting the calculations involved. The first and undoubtedly dominant reason relates to the search for certainty. Once someone, perhaps from within the marketing department, suggests calculating customer profitability, the gainsayers quickly and vociferously become apparent: 'How will we accurately allocate fixed and variable costs?' 'How should we ascribe the costs of operations and customer service?' 'How will we recognize the costs of different distribution channels?' All are valid questions and, indeed, there are many more issues that will require discussion and resolution prior to agreeing an appropriate model of customer profitability. However, none is insurmountable and many are simply red herrings.

Relativity is Key

Customer profitability is important because it recognizes and quantifies the indisputable fact that there are, in practically every business, major differences between the relative values of the various customers that the company serves. Recognizing and accepting this fact determines that they should be managed in different ways, with different levels of investment and resource. Of course, it would be ideal if profitability could be calculated to the penny, but life is not like that and in the absence of precision, relativity is often the key.

In most cases, it is more than sufficient for strategy-development purposes to know that one customer group has an *approximate* lifetime value of £100, while another is valued at nearer £300 or £50. Obviously, the less exact the calculation and the smaller the differences in value between customer groups, the less useful the tool becomes. However, the not unnatural desire for precision by (largely, but not exclusively) finance professionals has unwittingly stifled many a customer-value initiative at birth.

Complexity and Consensus

The second reason for avoiding measurement calculations relates to complexity and the development of consensus among the various interested parties within any business. One market-leading life assurer commissioned consultants to segment its customers according to their profitability. It took three months to broker a common view between marketers, accountants and actuaries of how profitability in the life industry could, and should, be defined prior to the analysis and strategy-development process even starting.

The Potential Benefits

Nevertheless, the effort is more than worthwhile. Just imagine what a difference you could make to your business if you could identify those customers who are adding value, as well as those who are taking it away. It would influence your market segmentation. It would help determine which customers you should acquire – and which you should avoid. It would help develop more profitable product and service propositions. It would help allocate a relevant and affordable level of service. It would help identify which, if any, customers to divest. It would help target customers for up-selling and cross-selling.

The range of strategic benefits is enormous and this list barely scratches the surface. However, few companies even attempt the task, relying instead on outdated and inappropriate accounting-derived measures that simply do not reflect the challenges, and opportunities, of customer management today.

Some Customer Truisms

In 1994, a well-known international strategy-consulting firm developed a model to demonstrate how the profitability of customers increases over time. To 'base' profits, it stated, should be added increasing value arising from customer referrals to family and friends, further product or service purchases, the opportunities for premium pricing and reducing operating costs.

Some have taken issue with the observations about reducing operating costs and the realization of premium prices, a view with which we have considerable sympathy. Notwithstanding this debate, there is generally no disagreement that:

- Different customers contribute different levels of value to each and every organization.
- The value of an active customer generally increases the longer that customer remains active.
- The difference in value between the high and low performers can be very large indeed.
- The difference in the potential, but unrealized, value of customers varies significantly.

Recognition of these differences can have a major impact on the ways in which the various customer value groups ought to be managed and the resources that should be allocated to them.

If these measures are critical for any customer-focused organization, why is it that the overwhelming majority of companies are still primarily relying solely on accounting-based management information systems (MIS) for their patently inadequate market and customer information? Let's take a look at just some of the problems and difficulties that arise from the traditional methods.

THE FAILURE OF MANAGEMENT INFORMATION SYSTEMS

Historical Bias

All companies will have management information (MI) comprising historical financial information based on past corporate performance. Many will project this information forward in order to consider the future. Very few indeed consider this future with reference to individual customers or customer segments. If such analysis is completed at all, it is *ad hoc* and sporadic. This means that organizations have no established methods of regularly fore-casting the potential value of the customers they have acquired and whether or not they will perform in the same way as those acquired in the past. The assumption is always one of customer consistency, despite a massive body of evidence to the contrary.

Why is it that in times of economic prosperity the credit institu-tions lend with abandon, yet are always disappointed by the bad debt that arises as they expand their market reach? Why is it that companies acquiring new customers with a price- or incentive-led proposition are so frequently surprised by their reduced compara-tive purchase longevity and loyalty? Why is it that companies continually seek to reinstate lapsed customers, despite the fact that they are so often unprofitable to acquire and service? All these arise because the current MI is insufficient for today's rapidly changing and highly competitive markets, and simply does not provide the data on which more insightful customer-investment decisions can be made.

Business Unit or Product Focus

The MI will also typically relate to business units or, at best, product groups. Indeed, there is frequently a significant body of information about the profitability and value of individual prod-ucts or services, which is, of course, a legacy of the product-management systems that have dominated UK businesses over the last 50 years or so. The same is unfortunately not true for customers or customer segments. Consequently, there is very rarely any unified view about the absolute and relative profitability, or future profitability, of the various customers acquired.

For example, a customer buying one product from a company will be reported in the relevant product profit and loss statement and the consolidated corporate accounts. Should the same cus-tomer buy again from a different product group, it is extremely unlikely that the increased value, or potential, of this customer will ever be identified by the company's regular MI – this would only occur through special analysis, should it ever be undertaken.

Lacking Insight into Customers and Markets

The information provided by accounting systems is also far too superficial and is designed to comply with the Companies Act and accounting standards, not to provide insight into customers and markets. Consider the average profit and loss account. Customer performance is frequently recognized in one line, turnover or gross revenue. This may be tempered by some performance qualifiers such as bad debt or product returns, but both will be reported on an aggregated basis that gives no indication of which customers are influencing performance.

Consider, instead, the wealth of information provided about costs, a plethora of reporting captions that might include everything from salaries to postage. Isn't it surprising that so many businesses are managed with a greater focus on cost control than on the dynamics of the customers who are responsible for paying for it all? The unfortunate truth is that the MI used by the vast majority of companies in the UK today is derived from the reporting requirements for the average sweet shop.

Probe further into cost-related MI and there will be reams of analyses by business function, ascribing costs to functional departments such as operations or customer service. Corporate overheads will be notionally apportioned, as will the depreciation of fixed assets that may be only obliquely related to the function of the department or business unit concerned. Comparative analyses will show year-on-year changes by cost caption, the variances versus the budget and the percentage that each caption represents of total costs. All very laudable, but there will be little if any analysis related to customers and the changing nature of their attitudes, performance or profitability – despite the fact that they are the *only* source of income for many companies.

How many management meetings spend more time considering adverse variances in stationery costs than how to increase revenues? How much time, effort and cost are expended collecting and reporting insignificant data? Why is it that we have an obsession with monthly reporting, despite the fact that many key measures change only slowly or infrequently? These phenomena are undoubtedly as much a function of information availability as

they are corporate intent. In the absence of customer insight, executives are forced to control what they *can* measure, which is not
necessarily what they *should* be managing.

Linking Revenues and Costs

The typical managing information system (MIS) treats all customer
sales as revenues and all customer-support services as costs with
little, if any, linkage between the two except on a gross margin
basis. There is no information that tells managers whether there are
particular customers, or groups of customers, who are costing more
or less to service and support than others, or who are generating
disproportionate levels of income. Consequently, there is the not
unnatural tendency to regard all customer revenues as 'good' and
all support and servicing costs as 'bad'; which, in turn, results in
cost-control pressure and the constant need to justify customer-
related expenditure because of the lack of any observable relationship between the two. This can have a profound influence on the
successful execution of the organization's competitive strategy,
especially in markets where margins are tight.

Customer Aggregation

The aggregation of individual customer performance into product,
or business unit, revenues also leads to a variety of other issues that
militate against insightful customer management. For example, a
typical MIS cannot differentiate between low-performing customers who are consuming a disproportionate volume of resources
and their higher-performing cousins who cost comparatively less
to service, despite the very different levels of profit of each (Figure
4.3). Consequently, both will be treated identically although, obviously, they should be managed in quite different ways.

Customer Homogeneity

The aggregation of data leads to customers being reported as if they
were a homogeneous group in terms of their purchase performance
and potential profitability. While this is patently nonsense, it is
reality within the vast majority of UK businesses, even the very

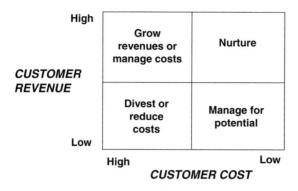

Figure 4.3 Customer revenues vs costs
Reproduced with permission of Valoris Ltd

largest that are often dominated by outdated MIS that preclude the realization of customer focus simply because the necessary measures have not been specified.

Balance Sheet Valuations

Millions of pounds are squandered each year buying companies because purchase prices are based on historical profit multiples and balance sheet valuations, when such calculations bear little, or no, relation to the current or potential value of the customers that the company serves today. Most due diligence investigations do not even attempt to estimate future customer performance and income flows, as this is beyond the resources of the seller's MIS and the capabilities of the purchaser's accountants.

So what *should* the customer-focused organization actually be measuring in order to avoid the sin of data aggregation?

TOWARDS CUSTOMER VALUE

The starting point is (perhaps unsurprisingly bearing in mind all that has been argued previously) the recognition that *not all customers are the same*. They do not remain as customers for the same length of time. They do not purchase at the same intervals. They do not buy the same products and services. They do not use the same channels and they do not all consume costs equally. Quite simply, they do not have the same value, nor do they have the same potential value. How each individual behaves influences the value they bring to the business or, more problematically, the value that they take away.

The Pareto principle really does apply and, in our experience, the 80/20 rule is often a conservative estimate of what is actually happening. In the travel-related business referred to in Chapter 3, 80 per cent of customers were generating just 4 per cent of total profits. In such a case, it is not difficult to envisage what a dramatic improvement could be made to company performance by quantifying the various customer value groups and managing them accordingly.

The Allocation of Resources

Once these simple, and self-evident, assertions are recognized and understood, the argument becomes significantly more straightforward. After all, isn't it obvious that the absolute and relative value of each customer should drive the allocation of resources so that customer needs are met, profitably? Surely, the argument is not *whether* value should be calculated and used to inform a company's customer management strategies, but *how*? Unfortunately, it as at this stage that everything becomes rather more complex. The calculation of customer lifetime value is, despite its apparent theoretical simplicity, fraught with difficulty when applied in practice.

Arguably, the primary function of any senior manager with responsibility for managing customers is to decide on the allocation of resources to maximize the return on investment. Or, to put it another way, he or she must decide how much to spend on each component of the manufacturing, marketing, operations and servicing mix, and on which customers, in order to increase revenues and profits for the enterprise and the return to its shareholders. Therefore, there can be no more powerful tool within the management armoury than the appropriate calculation of customer lifetime value; and no more powerful weapon than its successful application to the recruitment and retention of profitable customers.

Customer Value Defined

Over the years, customer lifetime value has been defined and calculated in a considerable variety of ways. It has been described as the sum total of a customer's gross or net revenues to date; the individual profitability of each customer subsequent to the deduction of appropriate marketing costs and business overheads; the projected value of a customer over their entire purchase lifecycle; the projected and potential customer value; or myriad combinations thereof, depending on each company's balance between the possible and the desirable.

In fact it matters little what your definition is, as long as the subsequent calculation allows accurate resource-allocation decisions to be made in order to meet your business objectives. While many definitions have been attempted, none has been universally accepted. All, however, include one or more of the following elements:

- *Historic value* – what a customer is worth today based on the profit, or contribution to profit, realized from their purchases to date.
- *Current value* – what the lifetime value of a customer will be if they continue to purchase and interact in accordance with their existing behaviour patterns.
- *Potential additional value* – what the customer might be worth if their behaviour could be modified to replicate the purchase and interaction patterns of more profitable customers.

What is Value?

Such definitions beg the inevitable question: 'What is value?' Herein lies the difficulty, because the answer is: 'It depends.' Some simple examples illustrate the point. Consider the manager whose primary objective is to retain the most valuable customers and protect them from predatory competitive poaching. Is it relevant to consider the sunk costs of customer acquisition? Consider the objective to maximize cross-sales. Does the value of previous core business sales matter? Consider a business with high fixed costs. Is it appropriate to allocate a proportion of such costs against the value of each new customer acquired? Maybe, maybe not; it all depends on what you are trying to achieve and the use to which the calculations will be put.

So the first and perhaps most important observation is that 'value' is a relative concept and will vary depending on your objectives and market dynamics. This ambiguity is the cause of most of the difficulties experienced by those charged with its calculation. Without a clear framework and set of objectives, every calculation will be wrong for somebody within your business and you are likely to remain mired in politics, almost from day one.

The Customer Value Matrix

Most customer managers are less concerned by the past than by the future. The fact that a customer has been consistently profitable in previous years is probably of less use and value than the forecast that they will remain so in the future. Similarly, most organizations market multiple products or services and, therefore, the likelihood of future cross-sales or up-sales is probably a key driver of future profitability. It is for this reason that the calculation of customer lifetime value must begin with an analysis of current and potential additional value (Figure 4.4).

Such an approach allows for the identification of 'directional' strategies. For example, customers with high current value, but low potential value, are obviously worth retaining. However, your investment in developing future cross/up-sales for customers with

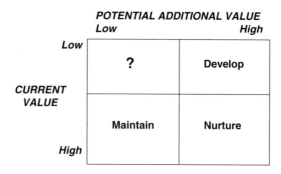

Figure 4.4 The customer value matrix
Reproduced with permission of Valoris Ltd

low current and potential value should probably be limited, as should the allocation of marketing resources.

Is Customer Lifetime Value Sufficient?

While the calculation of current and potential value is a useful starting point, communicating with all the customers within each value group in an identical fashion is unlikely to prove successful. Despite the fact that they exhibit similar financial value, the customers will not be homogeneous. They may have different demographic or psychographic profiles; they may have different requirements for service; or they may appreciate different aspects of your brand, product functionality or service features. The key is, therefore, to differentiate between customers in order to create a manageable number of segments for which cost-effective strategies can be defined (Figure 4.5).

The picture is further complicated by the fact that each customer, regardless of their value, potential value, needs or characteristics, may be at a different stage in their purchase lifecycle. Quite obviously, the ways in which you will choose to manage a high-value, recently acquired customer should be very different to your management of a customer of the same value who is already a proven loyalist, or one showing signs of dissatisfaction or defection.

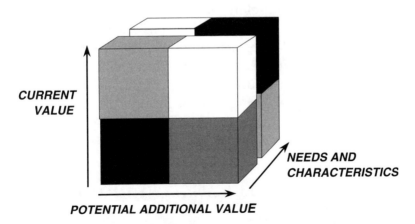

Figure 4.5 The customer value management cube
Reproduced with permission of Valoris Ltd

So customer lifetime value, while critical, is only the starting point for the development of a customer-management strategy designed to maximize the return on your customer investment. Notwithstanding these caveats, what guidance can be provided?

Some Customer Value Guidelines

It is impossible within a book such as this to provide a detailed instruction manual for the calculation of customer lifetime value – the differences between companies and industries are simply too diverse. However, it is possible to give some broad guidelines.

Let's start with current value. This calculation is dependent on not only your own definition of value but, importantly, on the analysis of where each customer is within their purchase lifecycle. This, in turn, is reliant on a thorough understanding of customer attrition patterns, as well as the ability to identify and differentiate between the characteristics and motivations that determine purchase and lapse behaviour. Unless you are able to meet these minimum requirements, any customer lifetime value calculation is likely to be based on averages, which is the curse of successful customer management. As has been said, 'average' customers only exist for convenience and because of the past inadequacies of management information, analysis and implementation systems.

So what is future potential value? This is somewhat harder to specify because it will depend on the industry and the product or service portfolio of the selling company. For example, the future potential value of a business airline passenger might be their propensity to upgrade their usual flying class, or perhaps use the airline for leisure purposes. For a bank, it might be the customer's propensity to take an overdraft or a loan, or start a savings account. For a credit-card issuer, it might be the likelihood of cardholders to use their card more frequently, increase their incidence of roll-over credit usage or recommend a friend.

CUSTOMER VALUE ANALYSIS IN ACTION

One general insurer was faced with all these issues. The way in which the company ultimately decided to calculate customer value is illustrated in Figure 4.6.

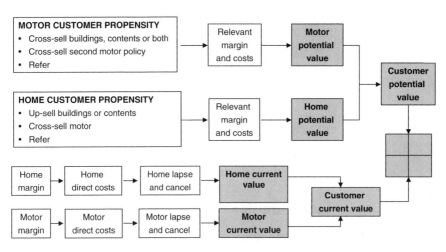

Figure 4.6   Calculating customer value
Reproduced with permission of Valoris Ltd

The organization had two main products within its portfolio, motor and home insurance policies, both of which could be sold individually or cross-sold to the policy holders of the other. Equally, both could be up-sold by, for example, adding a further driver to the motor policy or increasing the value of household contents cover. So the starting point was agreement on the purpose to which the value calculations would be put. In this case, the objective was to increase the profitability of the existing customer base, and thus it was decided to ignore the costs of customer acquisition in the current value calculation.

Calculating Current Value

The components of current value were therefore determined to be as follows:

- *The margin* realized on the sale of each product. This, in turn, was agreed to be a function of the premium income (i.e. the price paid by each customer) less the costs of all claims, plus the administrative overheads incurred as a direct result of such claims.
- *Less the direct costs* relating to ongoing customer maintenance, such as the costs of customer service and policy renewal.

- *Multiplied by the expected purchase lifecycle,* which was calculated by determining each customer's propensity to lapse, or cancel, their policy based on the historic attrition patterns of similar customers. It was agreed that a maximum of five years would be used because the environment was simply too uncertain to make investment decisions based on income assumptions of any greater duration.
- *Brought back to today's value,* using net present value calculations based on an appropriate discount rate.

Calculating Potential Additional Value

Potential additional value was determined using propensity modelling. The principles were the same for each product and included calculations based on each customer's likelihood to:

- *Buy a cross-sold product,* such as a motor customer purchasing a home insurance product.
- *Buy an up-sold product,* such as a second policy.
- *Refer a new customer.* This company had thoughtfully identified all policyholders acquired via direct customer referral. In this way, it was also able to factor the lifetime value of recommended customers into its future potential value model.

These propensity models were then overlaid with the relevant margins and costs to create estimates of potential additional value, which then formed the second axis of the value matrix.

Needs and Characteristics

The third face of the customer management cube, needs and characteristics, does not necessarily or directly have an impact on customer value. Rather, this facet of the analysis should be used to describe, and differentiate between, the various value groups and is discussed in more detail in the next chapter. The value analysis enables priorities to be established and resources to be allocated. The identification of needs and characteristics informs the customer manager as to how, when and (perhaps) through which media this value should be realized.

Segmenting the Value Groups

While the customer lifetime value calculations were important, it was believed that the primary advantages of such analyses would only be achieved if the resulting investment-allocation decisions could be reinforced through enhanced insight into customers, so that propositions and messages could be tailored accordingly.

A fascinating picture emerged (Figure 4.7). For example, 40 per cent of customers had a current value of £5 and a potential future value of £31. Conversely, nearly one-third of customers had a combined value of over £240. Quite obviously, each customer group demanded differing levels of investment. However, the question remained as to how such customers should be managed to recognize their differences and realize their value.

In this particular case, differences by income and age were identified. This was useful, but perhaps insufficiently discriminatory for the development of discrete customer-management strategies. The analysis did become particularly powerful, however, when attitudes, age and income were overlaid onto each of the current and potential value segments (Figure 4.8).

At a stroke, the possibilities for differentiation through creative customer management became obvious. It could not only be

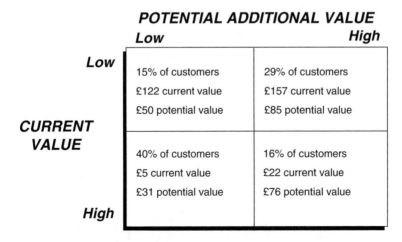

Figure 4.7 Segmented lifetime values
Reproduced with permission of Valoris Ltd

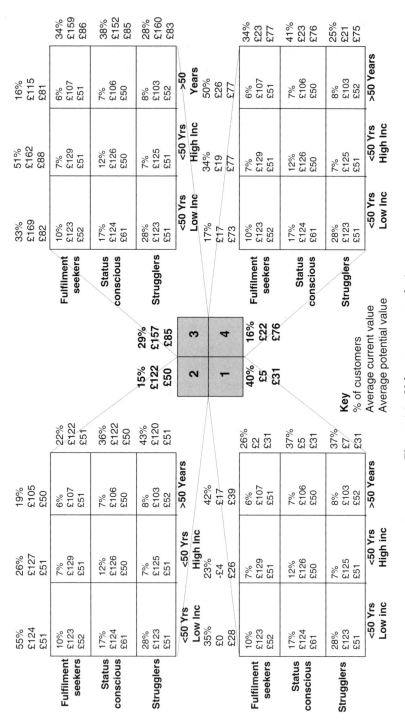

Figure 4.8   Value segment analysis
Reproduced with permission of Valoris Ltd

decided immediately where resources should be apportioned but also, and equally importantly, it could be seen that there were significant sub-segments with diverse personal needs that would be motivated by different propositions and communications.

THE PITFALLS AND PROBLEMS

So what are the pitfalls and problems associated with the calculation and application of customer lifetime value analyses?

Accounting Systems

The problem most frequently encountered is the inability of accounting-based legacy systems to manage and report on the ensuing complexity. Quite obviously, even if the analyses result in a relatively small number of discernible customer segments, each must be managed in different ways if their value, and potential value, is to be realized. Unless MIS are in place to implement and measure the various customer strategies required, all the hard work will have been in vain.

Clarity of Objectives

As previously argued, the means of calculating lifetime value for customer-acquisition purposes might be very different to that for customer retention, up-sales or cross-sales. Indeed, it may be necessary to calculate and employ a variety of different models depending on the use that is to be made of the resulting information.

The Necessity of Segmentation

While the calculation and application of customer lifetime value are essential activities, unless customers are segmented and the needs and characteristics of the various groups identified, the insight will be significantly less valuable than it might be. It cannot be said frequently enough that average customers simply do not exist.

Organizational Commitment

Customer managers might get very excited by their calculations and the strategies that these suggest. However, unless financial staff and senior managers are equally convinced of the validity of the analyses, the resources required to implement the resulting plans will simply not become available. Similarly, for example, unless customer service staff are committed to recognizing the differences between customers, understand their role in servicing them appropriately and have the necessary tools and skills at their disposal, the effort will have been worthless.

The Search for Certainty

Although the drive for a foolproof calculation of customer lifetime value is to be applauded, it is frequently impossible to be absolutely certain of *all* the costs and *all* the revenues. In such circumstances, it is more important to ensure a consistent approach and to consider the *relative* differences between customer values. For example, if one customer or group of customers has a current and potential value of £200 while another has a value of £30, the relative difference is enough to make the necessary decisions about resource allocation, even if both calculations have a possible error margin of plus or minus 20 per cent. Absolute accuracy becomes more important the closer the various customers or segments are in value, but the realities of the Pareto principle will ensure that there is usually sufficient difference on which to base informed decisions. Paralysis by analysis is often the death of otherwise perfectly valid customer-focused strategies built on lifetime value.

Abdication

Finally, perhaps the most heinous sin of all is abdicating the calculation of customer lifetime value to data analysts. Data analysts are obviously essential but frequently they do not possess the commercial skills and experience required to complete analyses of this kind. The purpose of customer lifetime value analysis is to set strategy and allocate resources. Therefore, the calculations must not only be statistically robust, but must also be designed to produce customer insight, as well as actionable and cost-effective marketing plans. The basis of the axes selected for segmentation and value computation are critical and require the input of experienced, customer-focused managers who will be charged with the responsibility for designing and implementing the plans that will emerge.

THE BENEFITS OF VALUE-BASED MANAGEMENT

Despite the problems and pitfalls, the benefits and advantages render value-based management an essential effort in today's competitive environment.

Investment Certainty

It enables resources and investment-allocation decisions to be made with greater certainty, and targeted at those customers who will generate the greatest value for the organization and its shareholders.

Competitive Advantage

It forces the recognition that not all customers are equal. Not only do they have different values, but they also have different needs and characteristics. When these are combined, the opportunities for the creation of differentiation and competitive advantage are immediately more apparent.

Credibility

It provides greater credibility for the customer management function, by involving financial (and other) staffs in the specification and calculation of value and by reinforcing its role as a value creator.

Innovation

It stimulates innovation, by forcing managers and staff to confront the differences between customers, thereby fostering greater customer focus within the entire organization.

Segment Budgets

It allows affordable customer-acquisition budgets to be set for each customer value segment in recognition of their differing levels of profitability.

Efficiency and Effectiveness

It improves the efficiency and effectiveness of customer acquisition. By understanding the values and characteristics of profitable and unprofitable customers, new prospects can be identified and targeted with greater certainty.

Customer lifetime value analysis is a powerful concept, perhaps *the* most powerful tool within any customer-focused manager's armoury. However, while financial analysis and mathematics both have an important part to play, they are insufficient on their own and, unless they are combined with expertise and experience, may serve to confuse rather than illuminate. It is tempting to consider customer value computations *in anticipation of strategy*. Nevertheless, the greatest gains are made by those companies that recognize that customer lifetime value, strategy development and segmentation are best developed using an iterative process, with each informing the other.

Chapter 5

Don't Keep It Too Simple, Stupid
The Need for a Segmented Approach

The more intelligence one has the more people one finds original. Commonplace people see no difference between men.

Blaise Pascal (1623–62)

A major supplier of commercial foreign-exchange services was concerned that the possible adoption of the euro by the UK government might have a catastrophic effect on its business. What could the company do that would enable it to quantify the threat that the single currency posed? How could it manage its business profitably if its primary source of income were eradicated at a stroke by forces outside its control?

At first glance the picture did indeed look serious – and potentially terminal. Its customer base comprised exclusively UK businesses, the vast majority of which were trading with companies based in countries that had joined the single currency or were forecast to do so. Customer attrition was not measured but was believed to be growing rapidly; and the average transaction value appeared to be decreasing. However, customer purchase and value analyses revealed an interesting picture that enabled the company not only to survive, but to develop a strategy that repositioned it for the emerging economic order.

It was true that the company's customer base, when considered as a whole, would become unprofitable if and when sterling was abolished, but value-based segmentation revealed a more promising picture.

A great many of the customer organizations with which the company was dealing were, in fact, simply testing its services, using it once and then moving on to cheaper or more aggressive competitors. The business's growth goals, customer proposition and sales-force incentive scheme were all designed to acquire as many new customers as possible. Before the threat of the euro, it was making very respectable returns and consequently its strategy was simple: more of the same and as quickly as possible. However, it was haemorrhaging customers so quickly that one manager opined that the sales force would have to be many thousand strong if it were to meet its turnover targets over the subsequent three years. This was obviously unaffordable, unsustainable and way out of kilter with competitors.

In addition, many of its customers were dealing in very low foreign-exchange transaction values, which reduced margins through increased costs and the loss of economies of scale. If this were not bad enough, it quickly became apparent that these low-value customers were among the most loyal and enduring. The longer they remained active, the lower average transaction values would sink.

This picture of a transient, disloyal and unattractive customer base was leavened, however, by the identification of a variety of much smaller but potentially extremely valuable customer segments. Hidden away and subsumed by the 'average' were a significant number of customers who were primarily, or exclusively, dealing in US dollars or other currencies unaffected by the introduction of the euro. Analysis revealed that these groups could also be further sub-divided into regular, low-value traders and more infrequent, but significantly more valuable, high-value businesses.

The strategy became clear. The company needed to pre-qualify new customers to avoid those trading infrequently, at low values and in the currencies that would be replaced by the euro. It had to maximize and 'milk' the business it had already secured with the higher-value European currency traders that would soon be lost through force of circumstance. It must seek to find and acquire more customer companies dealing in primarily dollars and other non-euro currencies. And it must retain the comparatively few, highly profitable dollar (and other) transactors that it had already secured, tailoring its customer-contact strategy, and its timing, to maximize the opportunities afforded by their established or pre-ferred trading patterns.

Had the organization relied on its traditional, unsegmented approach to customer analysis, it would undoubtedly have con-cluded that it must sell the business or even, perhaps, close it down in anticipation of the impending losses. However, by adopting a segmented approach based on customer profitability and potential, this company reduced its sales and processing costs, became more targeted and efficient in its customer-acquisition activities, and concentrated valuable sales and servicing resources on those customers who were not only profitable, but would continue to be so in the future.

SEGMENT OR DIE

Customer segmentation is fundamental to business success in today's fiercely competitive markets. Segmentation based on value analysis is no longer a sophisticated luxury, it is probably *the* most essential ingredient for the development of a profitable and customer-focused organization.

Customer segmentation is also the cornerstone of true customer focus. Without an effective and practical model for dividing cus-tomers into discrete and manageable groups, any calculation of customer value will be worthless. At best, it will simply provide a misleading and superficial picture of customer performance based on the mythical average buyer. At worst, it will lead an organiza-tion into making fundamentally erroneous strategic decisions that may seriously compromise the long-term profitability of the enterprise. Yet it is our experience that many companies struggle to apply even the most basic segmentation principles, and very few indeed base their decisions on the quantification of customers' current or potential value.

UNDERSTANDING CUSTOMERS' NEEDS AND MOTIVATIONS

Ask any salesperson why they didn't make a sale and they will often say one word: 'price'. This may be a generalization, but it isn't too far from the truth. Yet if the majority of people buy for price-related reasons, why do so many companies try so hard to add value to their products and services? Why is it that customers don't move *en masse* to competitors as soon as lower prices are available? The obvious answer is that, of course, price is only one part of the equation. Some buyers are remarkably susceptible to minor cost changes, while others value different parts of the proposition, such as convenience, speed or the ability to use the channels of their choice. The key to success lies in knowing which customers are which; and then being able to differentiate between them with attractive and profitable products, services, propositions and communications.

A Credit-Card Market Illustration

There is tremendous competition in the UK credit-card market, especially since the early 1990s when new issuers entered the market from the US. These new competitors did not possess the high-street branch infrastructure of the established banks and were therefore able to offer an interest rate on the use of roll-over credit that was significantly lower than that available elsewhere. Almost at a stroke, the market fragmented. Some people immediately moved to the low-price entrants; others sought added value, such as Air Miles or cashback on their purchases; others still were inert and remained with their existing issuers despite the ever-increasing array of attractive incentives to take their business elsewhere.

As in all markets, not all cardholders are the same so, to really understand their motivations and attitudes, it is necessary to segment the market; quantify the size of each segment; understand how many cardholders are moving between the segments; and identify to which new segment they are migrating. Figure 5.1 illustrates how this market can be segmented as the essential precursor to developing an appropriate customer-acquisition and retention strategy and marketing mix for each.

The axes of this particular market-segmentation model were 'price' and 'added value', with each competitor ascribed scores based on their interest rate (APR) and the basket of benefits that they offered their cardholders. Each issuer's cardholders were researched in order to understand and quantify their reasons for card closure or for the acquisition of a new card.

The results clearly demonstrated the complexity and fragmented nature of what was, until a few short years previously, a market regarded as mature, stable and homogeneous. The commodity segment comprised issuers competing on price alone, with few if any added benefits. Many cardholders within this group were, unsurprisingly, seeking out new card issuers for price-related reasons, either the absence of an annual fee or a low APR. Unsurprisingly again, many were closing their card accounts for the same reason, which was evidence of customer sophistication and promiscuity. However, many more were closing for reasons related to the changing nature of their card usage, or because they were seeking the additional incentives provided by other issuers. Even among this low-price/low-benefits segment, price was *not* the primary driver of switching to competitors.

Only by understanding *market* dynamics and the drivers of customer behaviour is it possible to develop *customer* segmentation models and propositions that will be competitively successful. Market segmentation aids customer understanding and enables decisions about competitive strategy to be made with greater certainty and insight. The proposition required to attract a buyer motivated by price will, by necessity, have to be somewhat different to that for a customer seeking added value. A cardholder looking for the convenience or reassurance of an established high-street bank brand may, on the other hand, be unconcerned by either.

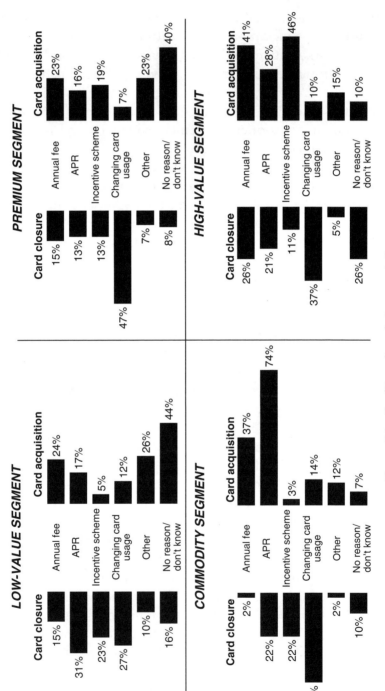

Figure 5.1   Credit-card market segmentation

Reproduced with permission of Valoris Ltd and NOP

Quantifying the various segments in any market will enable the *right* marketing, sales, service and distribution mix to be developed that will attract and retain the *right* customers – affordably and profitably.

Of course, who the right customers are will depend on the agreed corporate competitive strategy. However, regardless whether you are seeking to be different to your competitors, focus on the needs of particular customer groups or be the lowest-cost provider, an appropriate customer-segmentation model will enable you to target the customers you want, with an offer that will be attractive and motivational, at the time that is most appropriate for both the customer and your business.

Targeting Resources at Value

It also allows you to allocate resources more effectively, in order to maximize revenues and profits. One commercial insurance company needed to ensure that its sales force was spending the right amount of time with each customer based on their value and potential. However, the organization realized that the various buyers comprising its customer base tended to act in one of two different ways. Some were 'transactional' and simply wished to deal with the company when they identified the need; others were more 'relationship' driven, in as much as they were happy to stay in touch and maintain a dialogue, even when they were not actively seeking new insurance products or services.

The segmentation model developed by this company (see Figure 5.2) recognized the drivers of customer acquisition and retention in this highly competitive business-to-business marketplace. It also ensured it was able to provide essential information and guidance so that salespeople spent the right amount of time, with the right customers, in order to maximize the profitability of the customer base as a whole – even if this entailed disinvesting, or even divesting, those that were of low value or consumed too much resource.

Customer Lifetime Value in the Leisure Industry

The calculation of customer lifetime revenue or value is, of course, a vital ingredient if customer needs and behaviour are to be

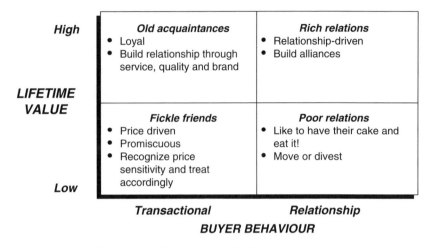

Figure 5.2 Segmentation by buyer behaviour
Reproduced with permission of Valoris Ltd

managed for profitability. One multinational company in the consumer leisure industry recognized that it served many different
customers, who bought at varying frequencies and had widely disparate values.

Initial segmentation analyses identified that the company had a
large number of low-value customers, purchasing relatively infrequently each year; and a few who were not only buying regularly
but also contributing disproportionately to lifetime revenue. The
importance of the few only became apparent when the absolute
value of their contribution was quantified.

As can be seen from Figures 5.3 and 5.4, 13 per cent of customers
were producing 60 per cent of lifetime value. And 7 per cent were
adding a further 26 per cent – another example of the Pareto principle understating the true value of the company's most precious
customer groups.

This analysis proved invaluable because, until the disparities in
value and behaviour were identified, all customers were being
treated identically. All received the same communications, at the
same frequency and cost, with the same messages and offers. This
was patently a waste of money, demonstrated a complete lack of
customer understanding and empathy, under-invested in those
customers who were truly valuable and over-invested in those that
were hardly paying their way. The communications programme

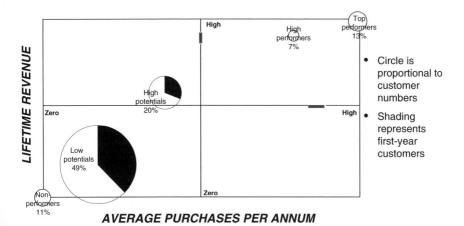

Figure 5.3   Segmentation analysis by customer number
Reproduced with permission of Valoris Ltd

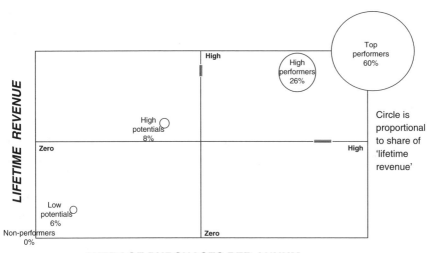

Figure 5.4   Segmentation analysis by customer value
Reproduced with permission of Valoris Ltd

was subsequently redesigned, value-related offers and propositions were developed, the servicing costs of low-value customers were reduced, and the return on marketing investment trebled, almost overnight.

So how do you get started? Segmenting customers typically involves six stages.

COLLECTING THE DATA

The first step is the collection of customer data on which the subsequent analysis can be based. In the past, before the development and maintenance of customer databases became commonplace, this was often a major stumbling block. The same is not true today. Most commercial organizations collect and store a multiplicity of data and the critical issues are now different and twofold: collecting and reporting on the right data that will enable insightful value-based segmentation; and, thereafter, maintaining it and assessing its accuracy, completeness and currency. Many organizations audit their customer data integrity infrequently, often only when a major data-analysis initiative is already underway. Mistakes and omissions frequently complicate the task and render the end results less than satisfactory.

The marketing director of a UK direct bank start-up was inundated with calls from potential new customers to such an extent that she took the decision not to ask for the source of the customer's enquiry in order to speed in-bound telephone sales handling. Operationally this was a fine idea, as it reduced call queues and allowed the bank to process more applications. In terms of long-term planning and customer performance analysis, however, it was a disaster. The company simply had no idea of the relative cost-efficiency of its various customer-acquisition offers and media, so future investment decisions were based on gut feel rather than hard, market-response data. It could not identify whether the customers acquired through different sources had different levels of profitability; and it could not assess whether there were differences in up-sales, or cross-sales, preferences or behaviour. The marketing director quickly reversed the policy.

FROM DATA TO INTELLIGENCE

The next step is data analysis. It is beyond the scope of this book to provide a step-by-step guide to data analysis and the techniques available to complete it. However, we will attempt some general guidance. The purpose of this stage in the segmentation process should be threefold:

- To calculate customer lifetime value and potential additional value.
- To identify the drivers of value: what it is that characterizes and distinguishes high- and low-value customers.
- To make insightful hypotheses about how customers might be grouped in order to improve customer focus, competitive performance and both customer and corporate profitability.

Customer lifetime value was discussed in detail in the previous chapter, so we will restrict ourselves to a discussion of the latter two goals.

Data Conversion

It is first necessary to convert the data into an appropriate statistical analysis package, so that it can be analysed with ease thereafter. This is typically where the problems of data integrity are encountered and it is prudent at this stage to build in time for data cleaning and even, perhaps, additional data collection to fill in the gaps.

The Initial Analyses

Once data accuracy has been established, it is then essential that the customer manager discusses, in detail, his or her requirements for the initial data analyses. One straightforward method is to develop a series of data cross-tabulations in order to look for relationships that could reasonably be expected based on experience. This can short cut the analytical process and avoid reinventing the wheel.

The list of possible cross-tabulations is only limited by imagination and the data available. However, in order to avoid being drowned in data, the ideal method is to design the initial analyses to search for the drivers of value. For example, do males buy more than females, or at higher values? Are there differences in purchase patterns geographically, or by income, social class or age? Are the buyers of one particular product more likely than those of another to buy further, cross-sold products? Who are multiple purchasers and how do they differ from single buyers? What are the differences between loyal, frequent customers and those who have lapsed or defected?

When specifying these initial analyses, it is worth noting that there are several truisms that provide a suitable starting point.

Purchase Frequency Increases with Customer Longevity

Customers generally buy more frequently, and at higher values, the longer they remain active.

In the example illustrated by Figures 5.5 and 5.6 from the mail-order industry, only 6 per cent of first-year customers were buying three or more times per annum. By the time they reached their fifth year, this figure had increased to 45 per cent. Looked at another way, only 5 per cent of the lowest-spending band comprised customers who had been buying for eight or more years, while 40 per cent of the highest-spending band was composed of such loyal customers.

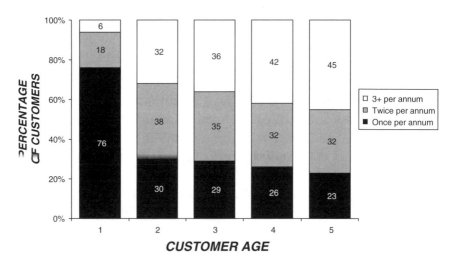

Figure 5.5 Purchase frequency by customer longevity
Reproduced with permission of Valoris Ltd

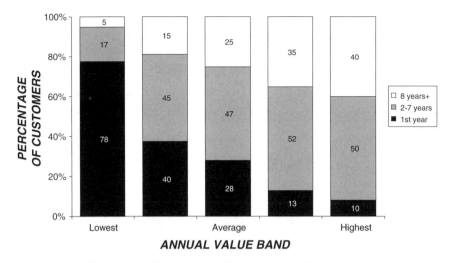

Figure 5.6 Customer age by annual purchase value
Reproduced with permission of Valoris Ltd

Purchase Value Increases with Customer Longevity

More often than not, the more a customer buys the greater the like-lihood of further repeat purchases. This is generally true for most types of transaction. For this reason, practically all customer files contain a large number of people who may have purchased only once or hold only one product; and a much smaller number who have purchased a great many times or hold a wide range of products. Understanding the incidence of repeat purchase, cross-sales or up-sales, and the characteristics of the customers concerned, aids comprehension of purchase dynamics, which in turn can provide valuable insights into possible segmentation models.

It also therefore follows that it is cheaper and easier to sell to multiple purchasers than to single purchasers, who are cheaper and easier than new prospects.

Customer Source Determines Lifetime Value

It is sometimes ignored, or unknown, that customers' values almost always differs depending on their acquisition source. A customer referred by a friend will behave in different ways to one who has responded by phone or post, for example. Such differences in value can have a profound impact on both profitability and distribution strategy.

Figure 5.7 shows a representative example from the travel industry. The value derived from each channel is markedly different and the investment made in each should obviously recognize this difference.

Attrition is Greatest in the Early Years

Brand preference builds over time: new customers are notoriously promiscuous. It is undoubtedly true that the greatest leverage over customer performance and profitability occurs in the first year when attrition is almost always at its highest. Some customers will be simply testing the product; others will be continually shopping around for the best deal; others still will suffer post-purchase dissonance when they realize that all the extravagant promises that were made to attract their custom were, in fact, simply hot air. The worst case we have ever encountered was a cable TV operator that was experiencing an 80 per cent average first-year customer-attrition rate. Had it not got to grips with the problem, it would have rapidly run out of prospects within its franchise area.

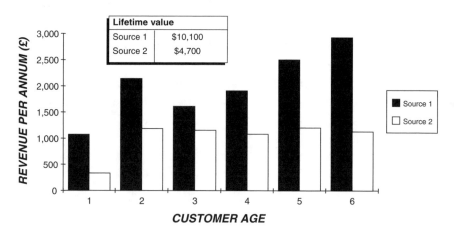

Figure 5.7 Customer value by source
Reproduced with permission of Valoris Ltd

It is a simple mathematical truth that the commercial leverage arising from making any substantial change to customer retention in any year but the first is usually comparatively minimal – and the higher the attrition is in this critical first year, the lower the profit opportunity becomes thereafter.

Identifying the customer-attrition pattern is therefore an essential ingredient of the customer lifetime-value calculation. In addition, it provides a clear and unambiguous indication of the timing of your customer-management activities and the performance improvements possible from any increase in customer retention. If this computation can be combined with an analysis of the *reasons* for customer defection, valuable insights into potential customer-retention strategies can be gained.

The Pareto Principle Does Apply

As we have already indicated, identifying those customers who generate the greatest value – and those who are contributing the least – is an extremely useful starting point for deeper analyses. Earlier we described a case where the top 20 per cent of customers were generating 96 per cent of profits. This is, of course, extreme; more likely would be an analysis that approximates Figure 5.8.

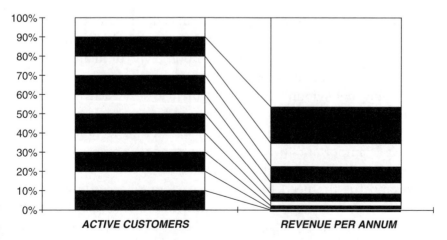

Figure 5.8   Pareto analysis
Reproduced with permission of Valoris Ltd

Looking for these 80:20 relationships is not simply 'nice to know', it is the springboard for further analyses that enable hypotheses to be developed about the subsequent management of customers. For example, are the most valuable customers those who have been active the longest, or have they simply bought high-value/high-margin products? Have they bought the widest variety of cross-sold or up-sold core products; or did they simply buy a high-margin add-on such as repayment insurance for a loan or travel insurance for a holiday? Are low-value customers new to the company, or is there a tranche of almost dormant customers who are active simply through inertia? Have they only ever bought a few products; or do they buy more infrequently than others; or have they simply bought low-price/low-margin products that depress their monetary value despite regular purchase behaviour?

These analyses can also provide the essential indicators of how potential value might be released. Understanding the drivers of value, and quantifying the various customer purchase behaviours that generate them, enables hypotheses to be made about possible segmentation models and the segment-based initiatives that will realize the hidden potential.

FROM INTELLIGENCE TO HYPOTHESIS

The third step in customer segmentation is the development of segmentation hypotheses. Detailed analysis, coupled with the application of both experience and intuition, will ultimately enable specification of potential segments that appear to explain customer purchasing behaviour. The task is then to test each in order to understand which appear most likely to be practical and successful. However, before considering just some of the techniques available, it is important to review the essential characteristics of a customer-focused segmentation model.

Foremost is the need to segment customers according to their value and potential value. The arguments for using value as *the* critical discriminator have already been made and need not be repeated. Despite the commercial logic, many companies still persist with their attempts to segment their customers attitudinally.

While there can be elegance in these models, unless such attitudes can be routinely and accurately collected, added to customer records and updated, they will be useless for customer communications purposes. Suffice it to say that the majority of businesses are run to make profits and increase shareholder value, despite what some managers might think or do. Profitability only arises from selling products and services to new or existing customers. The over-riding goal of every customer-segmentation model must, therefore, be to identify those customers to whom the greatest volume of sales can be made, at the lowest possible cost.

The European finance vice-president of a worldwide publishing company was arguing the relative merits of a particularly complicated marketing programme with one of the country managers. The VP was new to the business and found some of the practices he encountered to be overly complex and not focused on the right commercial issues. At a particularly heated moment in the discussion, he declared that he had found the secret of long-term business success: 'If we sell more books, we make more money!'

Even though they may have similar value and potential value, customers still differ in their needs, attitudes and characteristics. To complete the model, it is essential to qualify the value groups by further intelligence that discriminates between customers in a meaningful way. There is no formula for deciding what the third face of the customer value management cube (Figure 5.9 and

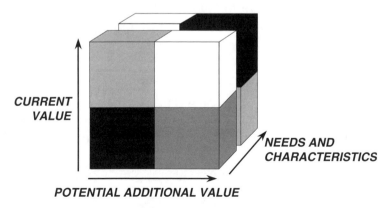

Figure 5.9   The customer value management cube
Reproduced with permission of Valoris Ltd

already encountered in Chapter 4) should be. It might be age, sex, preferred distribution channel, socio-economic class, or life stage. The key is to identify one or more factors that will improve targeting, proposition development and performance.

Whichever discriminators are selected, however, the resulting segments must fulfil a variety of criteria if they are to be commercially successful.

Homogeneous

Each segment should be homogeneous. That is, all customers within the segment should share a common set of behaviours, characteristics or needs relative to the product or service that they are being offered. This could relate, among other factors, to the frequency of their purchases, the number of products bought, the preferred distribution channel used or, perhaps, the customer's purchase life-stage. New customers may have very different needs for reassurance, information and service, for example, than their more experienced cousins. Lapsed customers may require the development of new propositions if they are to be persuaded to buy again.

Discrete

Each segment must be discrete. That is, the characteristics of the segment must be different to those exhibited by customers in other segments, and these differences must be significant.

Substantial

The segment should be substantial, so that it is capable of generating sufficient profits to warrant the development of specific customer-management initiatives and programmes. The 'segment of one' is a seductive concept, but is illusory and potentially extremely expensive and complex both to manage and deliver. In practice, customer segments must be large enough to be able to achieve an adequate return on the investment or risk involved.

Accessible

The segment should be accessible and capable of being identified, reached and served cost-effectively. One major UK bank decided to segment its current-account customer base and commissioned a well-known market-research company to help it with the task. Sure enough, the researchers developed a range of customer typologies that were both elegant and alliterative; the latter quality, for some reason, being seemingly *de rigueur* in the research industry. After six months' effort and an invoice nearing £100,000, the bank realized that it could not actually identify which customers in its database sat within each segment. As a piece of academic research, the work was impeccable. As a business tool that would help generate competitive advantage and additional sales, it was almost worthless.

Actionable

The segment must also be actionable, so that meaningful action plans can be developed that will improve business performance. This is where commercial experience becomes invaluable. Unless relevant and quantifiable objectives can be set for each of the segments, the model is probably inappropriate and useless. For example, it is perhaps self-evident that a segment of low-value/high-potential new customers should be nurtured and developed so that their latent potential can be realized. However, should a segment definition comprise multiple-product purchasers or buyers in a particular region, for example, it is less immediately obvious what the objectives for such customer groups might be without some idea of their value or potential.

Stable

The segment should be stable enough for customer-management programmes to be formulated with certainty. If customers are segmented well, and successful programmes are developed that demonstrably improve customer performance and profitability, then customers will migrate between segments. This is fine in theory, but if too many customers are migrating because the segment discriminators are overly fine, then the initiative may prove unwieldy and impossible to manage.

FROM HYPOTHESIS TO APPRAISAL

Once possible segments have been hypothesized, step four in the process is to appraise the various ideas to develop a workable model for which objectives and propositions can be created that will meet both customer and corporate needs. There are a number of statistical tools and techniques that can be used, including 'old favourites' such as factor, cluster and CHAID analyses, as well as newer approaches such as neural networks. Regardless of the methods used, the objectives are always the same: to validate whether or not actual customer behaviour reflects the hypotheses developed previously and to refine the emerging segmentation model.

Identifying the Reasons for Attrition

One very large subscription-based organization, with a membership running into millions, had hypothesized that customer longevity must be an important constituent of its segmentation model because of the increasing attrition that it was suffering in the earliest customer years. However, it was far from clear what was driving this attrition and the reasons, if found, would probably constitute an important strand in the company's customer-management strategy. Among other tools, CHAID analysis was selected as it allowed the analysts to quantify relationships within the data. In this particular case, the model was 'forced' to select customers according to the number of years of their membership. Thereafter, CHAID was used to determine which factors most closely correlated with attrition within each annual membership band. The results were fascinating, and wholly surprising.

That attrition was high in the early years was already known. However, it was a revelation to discover that the factor with the highest correlation with first-year attrition was the number of mailings sent by third parties to the customers during this initial, critical year of membership.

This organization was actually one part of a much larger group and the acquisition of each new customer was greeted with enthusiasm by a plethora of other divisions, departments and product groups, all keen to ply their wares to the newcomers. Unfortunately, it appeared that the sheer volume of (to the customer) seemingly unrelated, communications was taking its toll on the core relationship. This finding was subsequently validated by customer research, which indicated high levels of dissatisfaction among new customers with the company's communications practices. The importance of managing the customers' early years was validated and the company, at a stroke, had identified a crucial component of its future customer-management strategy.

Dynamic Segmentation

Another, very large direct-to-consumer company had proven over many years the critical importance of managing new customers well. However, yet again not all new customers were the same. Some were new to shopping in this way and needed a great deal of help and purchase experience before they became established, high-value shoppers. Others, of course, were already experienced, albeit with the company's competitors. They felt confident to buy at high volumes and values, almost from day one. Equally, the initial analyses had demonstrated that the frequency and value of customers' buying behaviour increased over time. A customer buying, for example, three products in their second year was exceeding the norm. However, should they still be buying at the same frequency in year six, they were patently under-performing. Figure 5.10 illustrates the hypothesis that recognized these twin phenomena.

The subsequent validation process quantified the size of each segment to enable the various cut-off points between segments to be established.

FROM APPRAISAL TO STRATEGY

Segmentation is, of course, of no value if the customer-management strategies designed to exploit it are not themselves

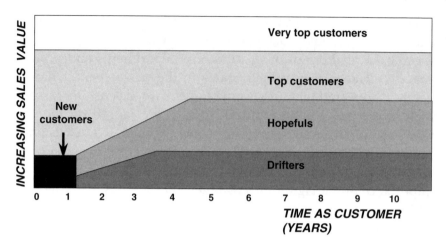

Figure 5.10   Segmentation hypothesis
Reproduced with permission of Valoris Ltd

segmented. The key, at this critical fifth step, is to ensure absolute clarity about the objectives for each of the segments you
are attempting to manage. Are you trying to retain customers so
that you can build their subsequent purchase behaviour? Are you
trying to increase their profitability by cross-selling, or up-selling,
other products and services? Are you trying to cherish customers
of proven value? Are you trying to reactivate previously profitable
customers?

Whatever your objectives, they should be unambiguous and
restricted to a limited number of complementary and practical
goals. Unfortunately, it is not unusual to see segment plans that
seek to retain customers, build their sales value and profitability, cross-sell other products and minimize the costs of service –
simultaneously!

It is essential at this stage to be guided by the customer-value
analyses. As the goal will (nearly always) be to maximize customer
profitability, objectives and strategies must be selected that nudge
customers' buying behaviour in the direction that will maximize
their value and potential.

In the example illustrated in Figure 5.11 from the commercial
general insurance industry, profit potential was contrasted with
strategic intent. The insurance company concerned was keen to

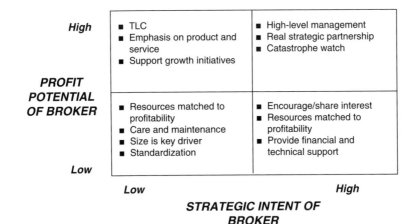

High

■ TLC ■ Emphasis on product and service ■ Support growth initiatives	■ High-level management ■ Real strategic partnership ■ Catastrophe watch
■ Resources matched to profitability ■ Care and maintenance ■ Size is key driver ■ Standardization	■ Encourage/share interest ■ Resources matched to profitability ■ Provide financial and technical support

PROFIT POTENTIAL OF BROKER

Low

Low   **High**

STRATEGIC INTENT OF BROKER

Figure 5.11 Segmentation by strategic intent
Reproduced with permission of Valoris Ltd

segment the brokers with which it dealt. It knew from experience and analysis that there were widely differing levels of profitability, and potential, within its customer base. It also identified a range of other factors related to the brokers' strategic intent that were important in determining how each might, or should, be managed. In this case, such intent was identified and quantified by the sales force and included factors such as the brokers' ability to sell on added value, rather than price; its vision and culture; its growth and record of innovation.

Those brokers with low profit, or potential, and strategic intent were therefore largely managed for cost minimization; while those at the other end of the scale were afforded a partnership approach, often involving the company's senior management in customer value creation and development.

FROM STRATEGY TO RESULTS

The final step is to establish whether the expected customer behaviour supports the segmentation hypothesis and model and is, therefore, reliable for future decision making. In the natural urge to implement the new and the more sophisticated, this step is often overlooked, or only attempted once the segments are in place, the organization has been redesigned and all communications have been produced. Unfortunately, what looks good on paper is often confounded by reality.

Customers are fickle creatures and do not always behave as expected. The fact that you have sought to nurture your newly acquired buyers and have lavished attention and resources on them does not guarantee reduced attrition and increased profits. A new competitor may have entered the market offering more attractive prices; or the economic climate may have changed since the analyses were completed; or your customers may not be excited by your new and improved proposition; or you may simply have implemented the strategy badly; or, heaven forbid, mistakes may have been made during the segmentation analyses.

There are many potential pitfalls and problems that may render your carefully crafted model and strategy worthless at a stroke, or certainly less effective than it might otherwise be. Testing is therefore crucial and omitted at your peril. Remember, until it can be proven that the objectives for each customer segment are being met cost-effectively, the model remains no more than a hypothesis.

Test and Validate Early

Make sure that testing and validation occur as early as possible. Look for ways to identify discrete samples from the proposed segments that are statistically representative of the whole, even if the process has to be completed in ways that are manual and labour intensive. Establish matching control groups of identical customers who will remain outside the test and act as performance benchmarks, and then test, research and measure. Are customers now behaving in the ways that you expected? Do customers recognize and value the changes that have been made in the way they are managed? Are there quantifiable and significant improvements in customer performance? Do increased revenues and profits justify the additional costs?

For example, one major consumer marketer decided to test reducing the costs of servicing its low-value customers by introducing automated telephone-handling systems. At a stroke, segment expenses were slashed and the customer service representatives were able to concentrate on providing a more personal service to those customers of greater value and potential. The strategy appeared to be working well, until a rapid increase in attrition was noticed among low-value customers. At first, this was not perceived as a problem because, after all, they were losing customers who contributed little to overall value, and retention had improved at the top end of the customer base. However, analysis had previously demonstrated that these low-value customers were large in number and made a significant contribution to overheads. Had the company rolled out the strategy, it would have been in danger of losing economies of scale that would have rapidly affected all customers and undermined its competitive position. Testing, however, enabled the issue to be surfaced early and the strategy was amended accordingly.

Segmentation Evolution

It is important to recognize that segmentation and testing are not one-off activities that, once completed, can be safely ignored. Customer behaviour will change, especially if the chosen segmentation model achieves its objectives. It is a sad but inescapable fact of life that the more successful you are at segmenting your customers and managing them for value, the more quickly your model will become redundant and need to be refined.

Similarly, it is unlikely that competitors will simply stand back and admire. If they spot you are gaining share, reversing share losses or becoming more profitable, they are going to want to know how you are doing it. While imitation is flattering, it also creates a more level competitive playing field that might undermine all your efforts and demand even more innovative or radical approaches. Consequently, the attitude of senior management must be flexible and supportive, with a readiness to see segments evolve as experience grows through the addition of further test results, new analyses and, most importantly, the quantification of segment profitability.

PITFALLS AND PROBLEMS

Testing is, unfortunately, not the only stage where it can all go wrong. Developing a successful customer-segmentation model presents numerous pitfalls and problems for the unwary. Nevertheless, none is insurmountable with a little thought and planning.

The Data Issue

Difficulties often arise because a company either has insufficient or incorrect customer data to develop meaningful segments; or, ironically, too much data, which can result in over-complex, time-consuming analyses. The unwary and the inexperienced both possess the tendency to over-analyse, in the vain hope that the answer will be in the data. It rarely is, which is why it is so important that the analyses should focus on the determinants of customer value, as well as the key drivers of customer behaviour and competitive performance.

The segmentation process relies significantly on 'hunch', born from experience, *knowing* what information is necessary to help explain different customer behaviour in a given market. Although data analysis can be highly informative, customer managers must continually develop and refine their segmentation hypotheses in order to identify the 'right' data for analysis.

The Incompatibility Issue

Difficulties can also arise from data incompatibility. Multidivisional organizations often have a variety of customer databases, one for each product group or business unit. While such an approach is acceptable when each division is charged with the sole responsibility of maximizing its own revenues, it can wreak havoc when a customer-focused approach is required.

Customer focus demands a single, unified view of the customer and company-wide agreement on the components of value. This, in turn, requires a centralized customer database. That is simple to say, but far more difficult to implement successfully when information-collection principles and practices may have evolved differently across the business.

The People Issue

In the drive for elegance and intellectual rigour, it can sometimes be forgotten that real people will implement the strategy and determine its success. In a business that only deals with its customers remotely, the problem is sometimes less evident and relates largely to the complexities of data management and selection. However, most companies use a variety of distribution channels that frequently involve retail or branch staff, for example. No matter how well you have crafted your segments and strategies, unless they are understood and capable of implementation by such front-line staff, the effort will have been in vain.

As a general rule, the more people involved in realizing a segmented strategy and the more distribution channels used for its delivery, the more straightforward and simple the segmentation model and strategy must be. Yours may not be the most elegant, powerful or even effective model available – theoretically. However, as in most business activities, doing simple things well is normally sufficient to achieve competitive advantage; and the havoc that can be caused by overly complex and unworkable models can prove a recipe for disruption and cynicism, among staff and customers alike.

The Over-Segmentation Issue

Over-segmentation can create dangers. Once the segmentation journey has begun, it is frequently tempting to push the statistical analysis too far, creating smaller and smaller segments of customers with increasingly fine differences between them. This is laudable in principle but will inexorably lead to inefficiency and mistakes. As the number of segments increases, the organization loses economies of scale and costs escalate. And as the distinction between each customer group narrows, so it becomes increasingly difficult to develop meaningful objectives and differentiated propositions for each. As complexity increases, so does the opportunity for human error.

SEGMENTATION: A POSTSCRIPT

A well-crafted and intelligently implemented segmentation strategy will go a long way to helping most organizations achieve long-term customer focus. It will also provide direction for the business by identifying the most attractive and lucrative parts of the customer base within which the company has the ability to compete. It will facilitate decision making and resource allocation. It will change the way the organization thinks about its customers, differentiates between them and services them. It will become the cornerstone of the company's competitive strategy.

Segmentation strategy development must therefore be pursued consistently and over a sufficient period of time to achieve the desired changes to customer behaviour and performance, which, of necessity, requires long-term senior management commitment.

Senior Management Commitment

Although relatively straightforward in principle, customer segmentation demands significant effort and investment. Data collection must be combined with analytical rigour, intuition and imagination. Critically, it also requires a preparedness on the part of senior management and all front-line staff to see customers differently. They must not only positively embrace the challenges that emerge as experience grows, results are achieved, and data quality and analyses improve; but they must also encourage the segmentation strategy to evolve and mature.

Organizational Commitment

Finally, it is vital that there is the widest possible participation in the segmentation-development process. Success not only depends on the application of a wide range of skills and disciplines across the organization, but also requires staff understanding, commitment and the provision of the necessary resources and support to implement the strategy consistently and effectively.

Customer segmentation is not easy, nor is it a one-off task. Once begun, it demands continuous improvement and development, which will have cost and skill implications that will, potentially, have an impact on all aspects of customer management and even the design of the organization itself.

An effective segmentation model is critical for the achievement of customer focus, but having an appropriate model is one thing: implementing it and aligning the organization behind it are altogether more complicated, but essential matters.

Chapter 6

Lining Up the Ducks
Aligning the Company for Customer Focus

If you buy the cow, take the tail into the bargain.

Old English proverb

After several weeks' negotiating, a keen sailor was on the point of buying a new trimaran from boat builders in Holland. After checking via the Web, she found that one of the two banks with which she had deposit accounts was offering a better conversion rate from sterling to the euro. As the account was serviced by telephone and post only, she not unreasonably called the bank to set up the appropriate funds transfer. Somewhat to her surprise, she was told that this could only be done in person, at a bank branch, because of the large sum of money involved.

On arrival at the branch, in a remote rural location (they clearly have not all been closed), much confusion ensued as the staff had never before handled a transaction of this type and scale. No problem, they assured the customer, because the branch had access to an internal foreign-exchange help desk that would undoubtedly be able to talk the local staff through the necessary procedures.

The challenge, however, was getting through to the help desk. The telephone number was permanently engaged. The branch staff did not know the name of anyone on the help desk and so were unable to use the bank's internal phone directory to contact the appropriate person. Not to be beaten, they called the bank's central switchboard and asked to be put through to the foreign-exchange help desk. After initially denying that any such facility existed, the switchboard then told the person calling that, unfortunately, the help desk was only for internal use and could not be used by customers. A somewhat surreal conversation ensued in which the staff member at the branch attempted to convince the switchboard operator that they were, indeed, a member of the bank's own staff and not, heaven forbid, a mere customer.

Eventually the caller was put through, only to hear a pre-recorded message that the foreign-exchange help desk was unavailable until later that day due to staff training.

The deal was eventually done, but not in time for the transfer to be made that day. And the favourable exchange rate? It transpired that there had been an error on the webpage and the actual rate was identical to that of the other bank.

It is tempting to believe that customer focus can be achieved simply by addressing those functions and activities within the business that involve customer interaction. Such a belief, like being slightly pregnant, is a dangerous illusion. Becoming a customer-focused business is a challenge that has to be addressed by the *entire* organization. Customer focus is not something that should be considered in isolation by the marketing department, customer service team or sales force. Even, and sometimes particularly, those areas of the business that have only limited direct customer contact must embrace the concept that the customer should be placed at the very heart of the organization's thinking and financial planning.

This is not a straightforward task and many issues and barriers will be encountered when attempting what, for many organizations, will be far-reaching change. Most of these challenges will relate to altering established, internal organizational attitudes, perceptions and beliefs, but many also concern the adoption of new ways of thinking.

ALIGNING FINANCE

The finance department may seem an unlikely starting point for building a customer-focused business. Nevertheless, there are three reasons for addressing it as a priority.

A Company-Wide Activity

First, there is a need to reinforce the message that achieving greater customer focus is a company-wide activity and will not deliver its full potential, and sometimes fail completely, if all business functions are not appropriately aligned.

Customer Profitability

Second, the simple and critical rationale for any business to become more customer focused is to increase profitability. Customer focus is about managing customers to maximize the long-term return on the asset that is the customer base. It therefore requires financial commitment and discipline. While all the skills and experience needed to effect such change will not reside exclusively within the finance area, gaining the early input and support of the company's financial community is essential. It will also significantly improve the pace of change that can be achieved and, if proactive support can be gained, provide objective measures of customer profitability as well as the programme's progress and effectiveness.

'I'm not sure how many customers we have, so how am I supposed to know how profitable they are?' This plaintive cry is heard all too often. Too few companies have any view of customer profitability at the segment or individual level. Yet such an understanding is surely the starting point for investment decisions about new ways of managing customers. Many business cases for the introduction of customer-management technology, for example, are developed without any real understanding of customer profitability. If the argument is solely one of cost reduction, such ignorance may be excusable. But even in such circumstances, there are dangers unless it is understood how the new ways of working will affect customers and the revenues they generate. Measuring customer profitability is not easy, but it can be done, given an understanding of the importance of the issue and a healthy dose of pragmatism.

Corporate Resources

The third and arguably the most important reason for involving the finance team in the journey towards the creation of a customer-focused business is that unless its members understand and support the commercial arguments for increased customer focus, the initiative and potential benefits are likely to remain largely unrealized. As guardians of the corporate resources, accountants are essential allies in the search for more profitable working methods, especially if they might require significant investment.

ALIGNING PRODUCT STRATEGY

Which is right: making what you can sell, or selling what you can make? Most textbooks will tell you that the correct approach is to make and deliver what the customer wants. Theoretically, this advice is sound. But anyone who has struggled with the issues of running a business and been around the block a few times will know that the reality is often quite different. Very few mature organizations have a manufacturing capability (whether the output is a product or a service) that is perfectly aligned to the needs of the customer. Even if this enviable position has been the case in the past, competitors, customers and the environment will all have conspired to change the status quo. In the real world, success comes from making the most of what you have and taking new investment decisions that anticipate the evolving needs of the marketplace.

New Product Development

The greatest opportunities for achieving increased customer focus in product strategy lie within new product development. For many companies, this seems to consist of a series of *ad hoc* project teams tasked with reacting to competitor initiatives or changes in the regulatory environment. There is, of course, nothing wrong with stealing other people's ideas, as long as it is done legally; and government intervention is a fact of life. Nevertheless, if these are the only drivers of a company's product-development activities, the result will inevitably be reduced differentiation, customer alienation and a gradual drift towards a 'me too' strategy in which competitive advantage slowly (and sometimes not so slowly) fades away.

To be customer oriented, products obviously have to be developed that meet the needs of customers, but simply meeting those needs is insufficient. To create new products and services that are truly customer focused requires creativity, imagination and, perhaps most of all, flair. These are difficult qualities to document in a process manual, which is one reason they are in such short supply in so many companies today. The sort of exploration and experimentation required to be successful often struggles to find a stable and long-lasting home in many organizations. When teams are created with a brief to explore new product and business opportunities, they are often the first to come under the axe if times get tough.

Cultural Barriers

Sometimes the challenges to customer-focused product development are quite subtle. A leading UK company with a reputation for a very strong, pragmatic, no-frills management style decided that it lacked imagination. It established a well-funded team led by, perhaps, the company's most iconoclastic and individualistic manager. So convinced was this manager that his managing director did not actually mean it when he briefed him to look for new developments two to five years out, he spent the first year building a short-term revenue stream that subsequently competed with the core business. Unsurprisingly, this alienated the existing product managers and eventually led to the demise of the new product-development initiative.

Appraising the Product-Development Process

There are many alternative processes for developing new products and services, as a trip to any business bookshop or university library will soon confirm. Each has its own strengths and weaknesses and it is not the purpose of this book to make recommendations on which particular methodology is best. Rather, whichever process is adopted, it should be judged against the following criteria to assess if it really is customer focused:

- Does it combine information and insights from all functions within the business that talk regularly to customers; and is such data combined with others from external sources to produce intelligence about customer, market and competitive trends?
- Are the financial implications of new initiatives understood, as well as being fully and fairly appraised throughout the process?
- Is new product development regarded and respected as a core business function, staffed with senior and high-calibre people armed with appropriate funding?
- Does it provide the space and opportunity for unconventional and different ideas to be considered and appraised?
- Does the process allow for the iteration of ideas in order to build on promising, but under-developed, new product concepts?
- Is the way in which competitors may react considered as an integral part of the planning process?
- Are enhancements to existing products and services recognized as an essential part of the mix?
- Are all the parts of the business that will be involved in creating and, perhaps more importantly, delivering the new products and services consulted regularly throughout the process?

Unless the answers to these questions are positive, there is every chance that the resulting new products and services will be less than customer focused, either because they fail to meet customer needs or because they will not deliver improvements to future profitability.

Figure 6.1 illustrates how such a process might look.

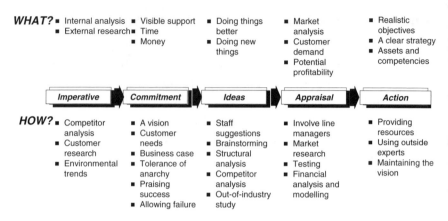

Figure 6.1   Customer-focused new product development
Reproduced with permission of Valoris Ltd

ALIGNING THE PROPOSITION: FROM PRODUCT TO PROFIT

The output of any development process is, or should be, more than merely the design and creation of a new product or service. It must specify the proposition, including a description of the customers for whom the product has been developed; why and when they will buy it; why it is better than, or different to, competitor offerings; and how it is to be packaged, positioned, delivered and serviced.

Even brilliantly crafted new products and services will fail to achieve their full potential unless the proposition is developed with the customer at the heart of the process, and there are many traps into which the unwary can fall.

Features vs Benefits

The starting point for most people considering a purchase is usually: 'What's in it for me?' This is the case even when it involves a complex appraisal process by technical buyers: 'How do I, or my firm, benefit from buying this?' There are few people whose first thoughts, when considering any new potential purchase relate to the features on offer. And yet time and time again, an organization's first line of attack is to try to sell features rather than benefits. Here are just a few examples:

- The computer manufacturer that advertises the fact that its PC uses a XG4090 video card, rather than mentioning the quality of the machine's graphics capability.
- The shampoo that we are told contains natural Cetartin, rather than the benefit that it makes your hair shine.
- The corporate travel firm that boasts it has access to the latest industry ticketing system, rather than its ability to source the lowest possible fares.

A Great Proposition – But for Which Customers?

Of course, what these examples illustrate is that propositions cannot be developed in isolation from a thorough understanding of the customers to whom the proposition is addressed. This will typically be one or more sub-sets of the audience for which the product was originally designed. So if the computer proposition above is advertised in a trade magazine aimed at IT specialists, it may be acceptable to refer to the type of video card, safe in the knowledge that the reader will understand. But if the same advertisement is placed in an in-flight magazine read by business people, it might well miss the mark.

Stating the Obvious

Propositions must also infer competitive advantage if they are to be persuasive. It is astonishing how many advertisements for watches and clocks lead with the alleged benefit that they keep accurate time. Is this important information? How many timepieces are on the market that *don't* fulfil this basic function?

There is a simple test for the validity of proposition construction. Just ask yourself: 'Why should I buy this particular product or service?' If the question takes more than 15 seconds to answer, the chances are that the proposition is not strong enough or, perhaps, is simply irrelevant to the needs of the customer. As soon as you hear the product manager, the ad agency or the salesperson reply, 'Well, there are many reasons you need to take into account . . .', you can be fairly sure that the game is up.

An Incentive to Fail

The use of purchase incentives to stimulate customer demand is a tried and, normally, tested part of the proposition. It would be unusual to find a business today using such incentives without having established the return on investment generated. What is frequently overlooked is the longer-term impact of such short-term tactical promotions.

Offering, for example, a travel alarm clock when applying for an insurance quotation will almost certainly increase the number of quotations requested and, if the conversion rate and the margin on sales are high enough, the arithmetic will stack up. But how does the inclusion of an incentive influence the attitudes and profile of the buyers? Does it make them more likely to become loyal and repeat purchasers, or does it generate new customers who will exhibit higher levels of promiscuity and defection? Customer-focused management demands that these types of issues are explored because the aim is always to maximize long-term customer profitability.

It is also important to consider what impact the use of incentives will have on the brand. If, say, the insurer is trying to establish itself as a sober, honest, reliable organization, does the use of 'cheap' incentives reinforce or damage these values? The manager tasked with, and remunerated for, the achievement of a new customer-acquisition target will no doubt argue strongly that the use of incentives makes economic sense. Such an assertion is easy to prove or disprove in the short-term when calculated in isolation. It is another matter entirely when weighed against the long-term impact on brand values.

This is not to argue that short-term demands can, or should, be ignored; rather, that even short-term decisions should be made with one eye focused clearly on the horizon.

BRAND ALIGNMENT

It perhaps seems obvious that a successful proposition must be aligned with the brand values of the business making the offer –

but it is also frequently forgotten. For example, the motoring organization the AA has attempted to transfer its very great skills at fixing things remotely to create a household repair and service business. If this proposition has yet to reach your consciousness, it may well be because the tremendous strength of the AA brand for all things automotive does not easily translate into fixing washing machines and central heating boilers. Conversely, the company has extended its brand with great success from a breakdown recovery service to car insurance and now claims to be the UK's largest motor insurance broker.

A Long-Term Task

Brand strategy must be aligned with more than merely the customer proposition. The brand, what it connotes and how it works must be at the heart of *all* product and service development decisions. In a truly customer-focused business the purpose of building and maintaining a brand and its associated values is clear: it is to assist in growing the long-term value of the business. Therefore, the investment required must be measured and weighed against the value that is created, which is not an easy task given the amount of time and money it takes.

There are a few exceptions where brands have been built at great speed. Examples such as Amazon or Lastminute.com spring to mind, but whether these notable exceptions are yet creating a positive return for their shareholders is open to debate.

In most businesses, building a brand is a long-term task that requires significant, sustained and consistent commitment and investment. Quantifying the achievable return on investment can be a difficult and imprecise science. It is always possible to construct a business case to support any investment decision, but differentiating between a forecast return on investment that is realistic and one that is illusory is a skill that is in short supply.

The Purpose of the Brand

At the very least, however, the case for investing in any brand must show how its realization and promotion will achieve some basic principles of customer focus. How will customers benefit? How will it reduce customer acquisition and/or management costs? How will it increase revenues, or profit, per customer? How will it lengthen customer lifetime? If these commercially pragmatic building blocks are missing, then the investment has to be questioned.

Naturally, the role and values of any brand will be particular to each market, industry and, indeed, company. But the approach to decision making about its nature and use should always be the same: to increase customer focus. That is, it must be financially driven and the leverage it creates, in whatever form that takes, must manifest itself positively in the ways in which customers think and buy.

ALIGNING DISTRIBUTION

When a business distributes through only one channel, life is easy, relatively speaking. Complications arise as soon as multiple channels and routes to market emerge. The so-called Internet boom at the end of the 1990s provided some wonderful illustrations; although for those who had been around for a while there was a feeling of *déjà vu* as they recalled the debates of 20 years previously, when the telephone started to become a serious communications and distribution channel.

Many companies saw call-centre productivity fall dramatically as customers sought an explanation for the different prices quoted on the Internet, over the phone and in retail premises. Airline customers failed to understand why a flight that was available through a high-street outlet was not available over the Web. Many customers were less than amused to find that an enquiry that began on the Web was invisible to the staff in the traditional service outlet. Much of the confusion was a result of the novelty of the Internet as a channel and the inadequacies of the new technology being employed. Much was also due to the failure of management to think through the challenges of multiple distribution routes.

To Integrate or Not?

The key decision for any multichannel business is whether or not to integrate the channels. Is the customer proposition one that states 'there are lots of ways of doing business with us', with the customer choosing which is most suitable at any given time? Or is it one in which the different channels are positioned as effectively separate businesses, albeit trading under the same brand? There can be no right and wrong answers, but customer attitudes, expectations and demands are usually the best places to start in deciding which direction to take.

Maintaining different distribution channels as distinct and separate entities has many immediate attractions. First, the technological issues will almost always be more easily resolved. Largely as a result of this, the set-up costs will usually be less. Depending on the degree of separation from the core business, different branding, positioning and pricing approaches can be adopted. And, of course, the new channel can be given its own management team with rewards and decision-making freedom unconstrained by the history of the parent organization.

It is very doubtful that First Direct would ever have survived from conception to birth and maturity had Midland Bank, as it then was, not had the courage to allow Mike Harris the freedom and space to plan for, and create, a business divorced from the history, culture and bureaucracy of the main bank. No doubt the positive impact of this separation was an important factor when, some years later, Mike persuaded Prudential to allow its embryo banking business, Egg, to be nurtured outside the confines of the assurance company.

Often, the hardest issue to resolve is whether the customers will accept the emergence of a new channel that is so different and distinct from those they have used in the past. Usually, the most visible manifestation of this dilemma is pricing. If prices in the new channel are different, will that difference be understandable and acceptable to customers, or will it be the cause of enquiry, conflict and complaint – often in alarming volumes and at significant cost? Channel integration, on the other hand, can be extremely demanding from organizational and technological standpoints. If done well it can nevertheless provide a powerful and additional contribution to the customer proposition.

The Fundamentals of Channel Management

Irrespective of whether different channels are integrated or separate, the fundamentals of channel management must still be applied:

- The economics of each channel must be understood. Which costs are truly variable and which are fixed? How sensitive to volume shifts are those costs? Are all the costs attributable to a channel correctly allocated? For example, is the cost of handling returns or refunds charged back to the relevant channel?
- The implications of channel cannibalization have to be explored. If a new channel simply attracts customers from an existing low-cost operation, what will be the impact on overall profitability?
- Will the creation of a new channel really allow the business to migrate from older, higher-cost routes to market, or will the company be left with all the fixed costs of the old channel supporting an apparently unprofitable customer group?
- Is the business really prepared to deal with *all* customers through *every* channel? Can such a strategy be afforded? If not, how are those customers to be managed who are, for example, insufficiently profitable to be dealt with face-to-face?
- Will the creation of a new channel lead to unexpected increases in costs? Creating access generates usage. The easier it is for customers to make contact, the more they will do so. As customers become more accustomed to taking advantage of the channels available to them, they will make increasing demands in terms of service standards, the quality of information they require and even greater levels of accessibility. All of these carry real costs in terms of volume capacity, training, technology, servicing and regulatory compliance.

ALIGNING CUSTOMER COMMUNICATION

Why do most consumer businesses (and some business-to-business operations as well) lavish their best brains, largest budgets and most expensive external advisers on people with whom they have never done business? Why, at the same time, do they typically give little thought, less money and seek significantly less expert external input when dealing with their existing customers?

If this seems like an exaggeration, consider two examples.

A Motor Manufacturing Example

Motor manufacturers spend a fortune on the launch of a new car. They shoot television advertisements in stunning locations using major Hollywood directors. They design and create elaborate brochures with glorious colour photography. They give opportunities to test drive the vehicle for an extended period, to practically anyone who shows the slightest interest. The campaign is usually brilliantly, and very expensively, implemented.

Then what happens once the car is bought? Nothing. No contact, except maybe a mailing to tell you that there is 'good news' because the prices of new cars are being reduced (so much for the much-hyped residual value when the car was being bought) and grief when it comes to booking a service that is convenient for you, rather than the dealer.

Of course, not all motor manufacturers are like this, all the time, but it happens sufficiently often to give pause for thought.

An Insurance Example

An insurance company launches a new product. It designs and writes an advertising campaign. It creates product literature, direct mail packs and fulfilment materials. Art directors, copywriters, account directors, product managers and marketing directors – maybe even the managing director – pore over copy, layouts, colour schemes and designs. They scrutinize every comma and polish and hone every phrase. The lawyers, the compliance team and perhaps even the actuaries make their invaluable contributions. The telephone number advertised is free of charge and the calls are answered quickly by obviously skilled and knowledgeable people. All in all, it is a masterpiece. The effort and virtue reap their rewards and new customers are duly recruited.

Imagine the scene a few months later when the customer needs to let the insurer know that he or she is moving home or wants to make some other change to the policy. The number to call is no longer free, but at least it is a local-rate call. The call is answered promptly, but this time by a recorded voice asking the customer to choose from five options. The inevitable, interminable delay is excused by 'your call is important to us and will be dealt with by the next available operator'. Eventually, the customer speaks to a real person who supposedly deals with the matter. The customer service representative does not seem to be quite as efficient as the people handling the initial sale and, when the customer takes the opportunity to ask a few supplementary questions, he or she is left with the distinct impression that the call centre operator would really like to finish the call as quickly as possible.

Two weeks later, when no acknowledgement of the call has been received through the post as requested, the process is repeated. Eventually written confirmation is received. It is a single, rather unimpressive piece of paper. There is a spelling mistake in the first paragraph and the grammar and syntax leave a lot to be desired. But it does the job – except that the confirmatory letter is too big to fit into the rather natty plastic wallet that came with the original policy.

Pragmatism or Carelessness?

The pragmatist may say that this is, in fact, the embodiment of customer focus: making decisions about managing customers that are profit driven. It is, of course, necessary to invest heavily to recruit new customers but, once on board, there is surely little need for the investment to be maintained?

If this state of affairs was the result of such a calculating and measured approach it would be easier to defend, although it would still be wrong-headed. However, these examples, which are astonishingly common among organizations across many industries, are usually the result of a lack of any thought rather than of great strategic insight.

Many firms will think nothing of paying for top creative talent to communicate to prospective customers while simultaneously allowing untrained and junior staff to construct their servicing letters. One market-leading giant, which regularly invests over £50 million per annum on customer acquisition, sent the same form letter to its customers *for over 20 years* until the mistake was identified. The letter was in response to notification of a bereavement and stated 'simply send us the name and address of your [spouse's] executers'!

An advertising campaign will frequently attract the attention of the company's most senior executives, while the thousands of letters that are sent out daily to existing customers will be invisible and ignored. The thrill of the chase appears to engage more attention than the hard work of husbandry, as Figure 6.2 illustrates.

Using Skill and Judgement

The fact is that every point of contact with the customer – from viewing a television commercial, to being greeted on the phone, to having a change of address confirmed – is an opportunity to strengthen the bond with that customer or to weaken it. The challenge is to manage these contact points in ways that maximize customer value. This is tough. Building test regimes around these multiple contact points can be expensive and complicated. What is needed, in addition, is some old-fashioned business judgement

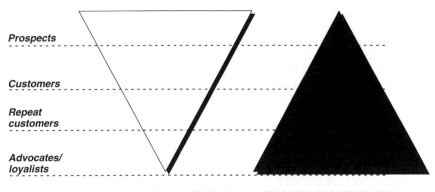

Figure 6.2   The customer investment/profit paradox
Reproduced with permission of Valoris Ltd

based on customer knowledge and personal experience as a consumer.

The key is to apply the same quality, and quantity, of thinking to *all* communications. Each point of customer contact should be viewed individually. The perspective of the recipient must be considered and the appropriate objective for the contact specified. All have to be done with the same precision, whether it is a modest letter telling customers about a change in servicing arrangements or a new TV commercial.

Communicating is Easy, Isn't It?

If the objective is appropriately set for the audience, execution can begin. The challenge at this stage is most business managers' belief that everyone is more than capable of writing a letter or holding a telephone conversation, so no special skills are required. The result is that the creation and control of most customer contacts are delegated to people who, with the best will in the world, should not be asked to undertake the task.

If this sounds harsh, take a look at your own firm's customer-communication efforts and find out who crafted them – and when. Not the press ads or expensive direct-mail packs, but the everyday letters and phone calls that probably make up over 80 per cent of your customer contacts. Lest there be doubt, this is not a plea for scripted telephone calls (which can have their place), but for telephone staff to be trained and coached in the appropriate communication skills as well as the necessary technical and product information.

If the wrong objectives are set or the execution is poor then, barring good luck, the only possible outcome is, at best, the need to expensively rework the contact because customers return with unanswered questions. At worst, they will simply go elsewhere.

This does not mean that Vikram Seth has to be hired to write customer service letters or Kenneth Branagh chosen to coach telephone teams. But it equally does not mean that these tasks should be delegated to someone with little command of English spelling, grammar or punctuation.

Finding a Common Language

There is an immensely successful Scottish direct-to-consumer business that is run on rigidly commercial lines. There is no place for sentimentality. It is a business in which the chief executive knows that it is his customers who pay the bills. He decided one weekend to take home a large pile of customer correspondence as well as the associated replies from his company. On first reading it seemed workmanlike enough, but he felt that improvements could be made.

He analysed a sample of customer letters and noted all the adverbs and adjectives that his customers used. He then read his own company's replies and similarly recorded the adjectives and adverbs. Imagine his surprise to discover that the two lists were very different. His company was, in effect, using a different language to that of his customers. Of course it was a language they understood, but was it a language with which they empathized, which spoke to them with familiarity? Undoubtedly not. He rapidly saw to it that his servicing letters were changed to reflect the language and hence the nature of his customers. Will he ever know if this was the right thing to do? Almost certainly not. Was it an example of real customer focus in action? Unquestionably.

This book has been arguing strongly that customer-focused decision making must be financially sound. Yet in this example no financial analysis was done, nor was it possible. But the costs were modest and the logic of speaking to customers in their own language was inescapable.

Communicating with customers is, in one sense, the most critical aspect of customer focus. Companies that communicate well, that align their messages to the nature and needs of their customers, that are clear about what they are trying to say and why, frequently exhibit the rather harder, more obviously commercial characteristics of customer focus. This may be because the managers of such businesses have the clearest understanding that it is *only* customers who generate true shareholder value. Financial manipulation, which sadly seems to so impress the markets and the 'teenage scribblers' (as Nigel Lawson so memorably described the analyst community), adds neither real nor lasting value, as has been seen with the Enron, WorldCom and Marconi fiascos.

LOYALTY PROGRAMMES

Loyalty programmes are one aspect of a company's activities that have only been touched on briefly, but deserve greater attention because they have become such a common component of so many firms' customer propositions, from credit-card issuers to supermarkets, newspapers to motor manufacturers, airlines to banks. In any one industry sector, direct competitors appear to take opposing approaches and many companies have changed strategy. Tesco and Sainsbury's do have customer loyalty programmes; Asda does not, while Waitrose used to but doesn't any more. Barclaycard does; Lloyds TSB does not; First Direct used to but doesn't now.

The mechanisms and incentives in use also vary wildly from company to company. Although the plastic card has become the near-ubiquitous symbol of these schemes, the ways in which they are used and how the various schemes seek to stimulate and reward behaviour differ markedly.

So what is customer loyalty and how do so-called loyalty schemes fit with the concept of the customer-focused business?

What is Customer Loyalty?

If a customer keeps on buying, is that loyalty? Do we need to know anything more? We do. A customer who goes to the same shop every day and buys the same newspaper might be loyal to the shop and the newspaper. But consider what might happen if the shop were to stop stocking the customer's choice of newspaper. How would the customer's behaviour change? If the customer switched titles without a thought, it might indicate that the previous behaviour was driven by habit, not loyalty. Whereas if the customer decided to stick with the newspaper and instead chose to patronize a different shop, we might infer loyalty to the title and not to the retailer.

The essential point is that loyalty comprises more than historical behaviour. While a long-standing record of consistent purchase from a single supplier or of a single brand may be an indicator of loyalty, it equally well may not. To be recognized as more than merely habit, there must be a combination of attitudes and behaviour that together drive preference and the repurchasing decision.

The reason that *real* customer loyalty is so critical is that it confers financial advantage on the firm that can create and keep it. When a firm builds the combination of attitudes and behaviour that produces loyalty, the benefit of such customer focus is a sustained growth in long-term customer value.

For some products and target market segments the loyalty displayed by customers can be significant. Motor manufacturer BMW is often cited as a marque that inspires almost fanatical loyalty among some drivers. But a quieter, equally profound loyalty can exist in less romantic brands. When Alliance & Leicester bought Girobank from the UK government, along with the assets on the balance sheet, it acquired an almost obsessively loyal customer base that, in both behaviour and attitude, was quite different to that of almost any other bank. These customers (or a major proportion of them) were convinced that in choosing to do business with the rather dull, certainly unglamorous Girobank, they had found one of the financial world's best-kept secrets. The reasons for their loyalty were complex, but included a set of features and benefits that were ideal for their particular needs, that fitted their lifestyles and also offered a public-service ethic that chimed with their own thinking. Sadly, this real but unrecorded asset was largely hidden, unrecognized and allowed to wither.

Loyalty is an inherent characteristic of the best customer relationships that goes beyond past behaviour. It arises when functionality and positioning combine to create a bond between supplier and buyer. So what role do loyalty schemes have in this mix? The short answer is 'not a lot'. The overwhelming majority of so-called loyalty schemes are in fact simply devices to stimulate repeat purchase. Not that there is anything wrong with that, but it is important that the two are not confused. The cleverly designed schemes create 'hooks' that not only encourage a particular type of buying behaviour, but also provide a disincentive to shop elsewhere – as anyone who has ever saved Air Miles for a particularly important trip will know.

Loyalty programmes come in many shapes and sizes, but they can be placed into three generic categories that are not mutually exclusive.

Reward Schemes

Customers receive tangible benefits, primarily from third-party organizations, in exchange for the desired behaviour. An example already mentioned is Air Miles.

Discount/Money-Back Programmes

Credit cards are perhaps the greatest proponents of this mechanism and of course many of the supermarket schemes provide benefits by way of discount offers to customers who collect their points. Some schemes, such as the Tesco Clubcard, combine discounts with offers from third parties, such as reduced-price travel tickets.

Recognition Programmes

In these schemes the benefits come from the operator in the form of product- or service-related benefits. Airline programmes offering free flights and the use of airport lounges are just one example, although most also offer benefits provided by partner organizations.

All three of these approaches have one thing in common. They focus on stimulating particular behaviour. They do not, of themselves, attempt to influence attitudes. Indeed, sometimes they can even alienate the very customers they seek to entice. Anyone who has attempted to convert airline points, to discover that the only available flights are at 5am, from an obscure airport on the third Wednesday of each month, will appreciate the issue.

However, when the benefits provided by the scheme are well designed and strike a chord with customers, and when the execution and management of the programme are of high quality, it can achieve a life of its own and, at the very least, start to build a solid base of repeat custom.

Loyalty schemes are therefore almost always inappropriately named. It does not mean, however, that they cannot play a significant role in the management of customers. The use of the term 'loyalty' for external consumption is fine, but managers must not allow themselves to be seduced into believing that the repeat purchase they are stimulating is necessarily a genuine reflection of altered customer attitudes.

Loyalty Programmes: a Checklist

Research by the authors revealed the checklist in Figure 6.3, which itemizes the most frequently occurring reasons for loyalty scheme introduction. The more positive the answers, the more likely it is that such a programme may be worthwhile.

Our research proved that many schemes are not launched as the result of a rational analysis, but as a knee-jerk reaction to competitor activity. Sometimes companies find themselves forced into such a move by City analysts who demand to know how the organization intends to respond to a competitive initiative. Schizophrenically, the analysts will also frequently challenge such schemes when they are perceived to be nothing more than the opening shots in a price war.

As with so much in business, however sound the rationale for adopting any particular course of action, it is frequently the quality of the design and implementation that makes the difference between success and failure. There are some critical, customer-focused principles that should govern the development of a loyalty scheme and will significantly improve the chances of success.

The Big Picture

If a scheme forms part of a clear strategy and is focused on the achievement of business objectives, the chances of success are

		YES	NO
1	Are competitor schemes prevalent?	☐	☐
2	Is the industry mature with little scope for differentiation?	☐	☐
3	Is competition concentrated?	☐	☐
4	Does the company have a large fixed-cost base?	☐	☐
5	Is product/service differentiation difficult?	☐	☐
6	Are customers' switching costs low?	☐	☐
7	Is purchase seasonal?	☐	☐
8	Is the average transaction value high?	☐	☐
9	Is the purchase frequency 1–4 times per annum?	☐	☐
10	Is the brand strong?	☐	☐

Figure 6.3 Consumer loyalty programmes: the strategic rationale
Reproduced with permission of Valoris Ltd

much improved. When it is 'bolted on' to an existing strategy, with little thought about how it will affect the rest of the organization, the probability of failure will increase accordingly.

Something for Something

Loyalty scheme customers carry with them real costs, both internal and external. The value generated must exceed the costs by a sufficient margin to achieve the business's risk-adjusted return on investment criteria. While this may seem obvious, many proposals to adopt loyalty programmes fail to recognize that there may be other, and better, investment opportunities available. The appraisal process should be rigorous and consider all the alternatives.

Some are More Equal than Others

The scheme must recognize that not all customers have the same potential to deliver incremental value. Those programmes in which all customers are managed in an identical way will risk over-investing in customers whose potential is already fully exploited. Customers at either end of the spectrum, both those whose spending power is limited and those who are already spending significant amounts, will probably deliver the least value. As with all aspects of customer focus, the shape and nature of the customer base are paramount.

Being Single-Minded

Failing schemes are often defended on the grounds of their contribution to some hitherto unstated objective, such as gathering customer data. Despite the fact that collecting this data was not necessarily a part of the original business case, and the ways in which it is to be used and how it will add value remain unexplained, the excuse frequently provides a welcome safety net.

Where's the Exit?

Loyalty schemes create, and alter, customer expectations. Such expectations may well expand dramatically when it is announced that a programme is to be withdrawn. The reaction of those customers who have been devotees can be volcanic. Equally, those customers who have hitherto shown little or no interest may suddenly feel that the ending of the programme threatens their very existence! The costs and mechanisms for exit are almost always ignored when the original proposal is devised. The most significant costs may not be those that are immediately recognizable in this year's profit and loss account, but they nevertheless destroy long-term value through customer complaints and bad publicity.

ALIGNMENT: A POSTSCRIPT

Customer focus can only be achieved if the whole of the business is aligned with the thinking and purpose that are integral to the concept. It is *not* the responsibility of the marketing department, the sales team or the customer service operation. It affects how the entire business thinks and is run.

The CEO and his or her team have to be the standard bearers. They must, through their words and actions, demonstrate that only when the entire business is focused on the customer will the benefits really begin to be realized. They must also ensure that the drive to create a customer-focused business is a continuing effort rather than a one-off initiative. In short, It has to become 'the way we do things round here'.

Chapter 7

Are You the Problem?

The Role of Leadership in Creating Customer Focus

He that diggeth a pit shall fall into it.

Ecclesiastes 10:8

About two years ago, a large services firm with £3bn of annual revenues failed in its bid to renew a customer contract that it had confidently expected to keep. As an individual account, this loss of business was not particularly significant. The account manager concerned lost some commission; her line manager gave her a hard time; and the sales manager reviewed how the bid was managed and what lessons could be learned. All good stuff. End of story? Sadly not.

A few weeks later, the managing director of the now former customer happened to give an interview to a trade magazine. To illustrate how dynamic his team was he referred, in passing, to the recent change of supplier as part of his firm's continual search for value for money. A week later the trade magazine concerned led its story with: 'Bloggins loses account through poor value for money'. The name is changed to protect the guilty.

Here the plot thickens. One of the non-executive directors of 'Bloggins' happened to notice the trade magazine article, tore it out and sent it to his chief executive with one of those ever so helpful notes saying 'thought you should see this'. To his credit (despite being embarrassed by the intervention) the chief executive did not rain destruction on the heads of his minions, but did ask for an explanation of how the bid had been handled and how the pricing decision had been made.

He discovered that, while there was a slick process to prevent under-bidding, if a bid price was within the guidelines set by the finance department the final pricing decision was left to the team in the field for all but the largest accounts. The logic was sound. The sales team was closest to the customer and in the best possible position to gauge the nature and intensity of the competition. The finance department controlled the lower limit for bids, while the account managers and their line managers had a remuneration package that gave them a real incentive not just to win the business, but to secure the best possible price. Nevertheless, the system did not seem to have worked – the bid had been lost – and the intervention of a board director meant that the chief executive felt he had to be seen to do something positive.

His first request – that the sales director sign off on all bids – was rejected when it was explained that this would occupy virtually all of her time. The debate continued and eventually sanity prevailed. It was accepted that although this bid had been lost, it really was 'just one of those things' and the company's procedures were robust.

If the story ended there, all would be well. The consequences were slight: a few hours of executive time lost and some angst among the sales team. But our chief executive was still unhappy. Nothing had actually been done and there was the outstanding issue of how to respond to the concerned non-executive director who had prompted the review. After further debate it was agreed that, while the sales director would *not* get involved in reviewing the bids, there was a need to ensure that, in future, everyone took greater account of the competition. Within the marketing department was a small team of analysts who, among other things, carried out regular surveys of the competition. In future, they would be required to provide input for all bids.

The result? The chief executive could now tell his non-executive colleague that, after careful consideration, positive action had been taken. Unfortunately that is not all that happened. The marketing department was keen to get involved and demonstrate that it could add value to the business. The marketing director was particularly pleased to have the chance to meddle in the sales director's affairs. As you might imagine, the sales team was thrilled. After initial skirmishes between the two departments escalated, the chief executive stepped in and decreed that he wanted no more debate or argument. In future, every bid had to be reviewed by the marketing department before it was submitted.

Six weeks later the new approach was abandoned and things went back to the way they had been before all this happened. The delays caused by securing the marketing team's input (not helped by the sales management's habit of asking for it at the last minute, or late on a Friday afternoon) caused some bids to be lost simply because deadlines were missed. Subsequently, relations with several customers became strained when the company failed to provide the swift response to their bid requests to which they had become accustomed.

What started as an entirely reasonable intervention to address a customer-focused problem had resulted in even more lost business, reduced customer confidence and increasingly strained relations between two senior colleagues.

This story illustrates how even the best of intentions can go awry, especially when initiatives that are meant to create greater customer focus are implemented in an *ad hoc* and unstructured way. A number of dangers can lie in wait for the unwary.

DATA-LESS DECISION MAKING

Most business managers would describe effective decision making (albeit using their own words) as a process whereby information is analysed and combined with both experience and intuition to choose a course of action most likely to produce the desired outcome. The starting point is, or should be, some facts. In the previous story, however, the facts available were limited, to put it mildly. There was no analysis of how often bids were lost, what their contribution to profit might have been, nor of the cost of the proposed solutions. Above all, the real reasons for the loss of the bid were never really ascertained. Furthermore, the desired outcome was ill defined; in reality, it was primarily to be *seen* to be doing something.

Over- and Under-Reaction

A business's ability to take decisions quickly and implement change effectively is priceless. Nevertheless, knee-jerk reactions can be costly, especially when they are initiated from the top of the organization without sufficient regard to what is really happening at the coalface. This is often seen in the customer service area. In many large businesses, particularly those dealing with a significant numbers of consumer customers, the reality is that senior management will usually only hear about major systemic failures, or about problems raised by customers who are known to them personally or by extremely vocal customer or consumer groups. Even though the Board may receive regular information about, among other measures, customer recruitment, retention and satisfaction levels, those events that galvanize the most action, and consume the greatest time and resources, will often be the one-off, big issues that capture its attention – or that of the press.

Sometimes, however, this high-level attention can be beneficial. Not too long ago, a major bank held an extensive and costly internal inquiry into a failure of its telecoms infrastructure, which caused several call centres to be off-line for several hours. This very public failure was reported in the national press and, understandably, deserved and received a great deal of attention, from the chairman downwards.

The upside of the catastrophe was that the head of customer service was able (after months of trying) to gain senior management's attention to the endemic shortcomings of the company's service delivery technology. Systems had been falling over on an almost daily basis for many months, but never for long enough to cause the sort of high-visibility issue that in one fell swoop would persuade the board that there really was a problem.

Of course, such large and highly visible issues have to be addressed, but the greatest commercial impact can often arise from the small, everyday service problems that insidiously infect the minds of customers over time. These include problems that make them less likely to repurchase, more likely to defect and, of greater significance, more inclined to spread the word about what a frustrating and dissatisfying time they have had.

REARRANGING THE DECKCHAIRS

Those of you who remember total quality management (TQM) will not need to be reminded that this was about the time when it became respectable for corporations to acknowledge that customers were important. Annual reports started to talk about the need to consider not only shareholders, but also those people who provided the wherewithal to pay dividends and achieve capital growth.

For many firms, inserting a few platitudes into the chairman's annual letter was where TQM started and ended. And for many such businesses this was just as well. Polishing the yearly reports to reflect the latest management fads did not affect the way the business was *actually* run. If the company operated as a monopoly (or near monopoly) or if the customer was locked in with onerous contractual terms, the future flow of profits was probably only minimally affected.

The real damage was done when organizations started to believe in the primacy of the customer without considering the consequences – and without being genuinely prepared to change the ways in which the business operated.

Imagine the scene: a crowded railway platform. The loudspeakers spring into barely audible life. 'Here is an announcement for our customers on platform seven.' Bewildered passengers stare about in confusion. Customers? Do they mean us? Fortunately, their minds are put to rest when the message is delivered, telling them that their train is going to be late, yet again. The novelty of their status as 'customers' is as short-lived as it was meaningless.

Time Well Spent?

But how many hours of meetings do you suppose went into the decision to call passengers 'customers'? How much effort was spent on internal communications and training? Would calling passengers by another name persuade them that, despite all the evidence to the contrary, things were actually getting better; or would it simply serve to irritate and annoy? Perhaps such a move would transform the mindset of staff and create thousands of happy smiling faces, all eager to make sure that the customers have a wonderful transportation experience? Perhaps not!

The reality is that such woolly thinking does real damage. It reinforces the customer's belief that not only is the service failing to improve, but also that the supplier would rather spend time on irrelevancies. The staff don't miss the point either. They know full well that no traveller in the history of the railways has ever complained about being called a passenger. The staff begin to question just what their managers are up to and become cynical and disillusioned when genuinely useful initiatives are subsequently launched.

THE PITFALLS OF PROJECT TEAMS

The first reaction of many firms to their new-found desire to focus on the customer is to set up a project team. This is fine as far as it goes, but it misses an essential point. Customer focus is as much about attitude as it is about process and procedure. Projects, which are often an integral part of effecting change, have a finite lifetime. If a company believes that creating customer focus is a one-off task, like establishing a new call centre, it will have missed the point. Not only will this sort of thinking fail to create a truly customer-focused business, it may also result in significant damage. While the project is running, staff will see activity and change. If the project is well designed and managed, they will become involved and enthused by what is happening. When the project ends, however, the impression can easily be created that what was once important is no longer a priority, that all the effort was really just about following this year's fashionable management trend with no measurable impact on customer behaviour or profitability.

Projects, and project teams, are undoubtedly needed, but there must be a recognition that customer focus is about the way a company makes money, how it thinks and behaves. It requires ongoing commitment, significant and constant effort and, crucially, the investment necessary to achieve lasting change.

BEST PRACTICE IS SOMETIMES BEST LEFT ALONE

Often seen as being of particular value is the desire to compare and contrast the organization's performance with best-in-class businesses from other industries and trade sectors. It is hard to argue that such an approach is wrong, and there are many aspects of business life where it can provide powerful insights and stimulate new, and better, ways of doing things. The keys to success, however, are relevance and context.

If a firm is considering, say, quality-control procedures within a manufacturing environment, there are undoubtedly many lessons to be learned from studying the approaches adopted by others across a variety of different industries. Nevertheless, the study must always be in context. The quality-sampling rates needed by a maker of baby food will probably not be relevant to a manufacturer of light bulbs, whereas both may be able to learn much from each other's recording and reporting methodologies.

Context is Everything

When considering customer focus, the context for comparison has to be, unsurprisingly, the customer. It is impossible to determine what is best practice without understanding the ways in which particular customer groups behave when confronted by different service approaches; and studying apparently successful, but unrelated, businesses to establish best practice is frequently extremely misleading.

A medical insurance company operated what were widely regarded as leading-edge customer-service facilities. Any firm looking to identify best practice in customer focus might easily have chosen this insurer as an exemplar. The conclusion would quickly have been drawn that its rapid turnaround of correspondence, swift response times and low number of lost customer calls represented the way forward if its impressive growth and profitability were to be emulated.

However, any firm simply copying the methods and approach of this insurer was unlikely to have been successful. The real driver of this particular company's success (something that had been demonstrated repeatedly by empirical evidence) was, in fact, its ability to advise its customers at the earliest possible moment whether or not their planned course of treatment would be covered by their policy.

The reason this issue was important is self-evident, but its overwhelming importance was a function of many factors: the age and social-class profile of its customers; the insurer's brand positioning; the complexity of its policies; and the relationship between the insurer and the medical profession, and how that was communicated to the patients. All of these combined to create a particularly powerful driver of customer behaviour. Any other firm (even direct competitors) reviewing the insurer and seeking to find the key to best practice was likely to have been mightily misled.

Seeking out best practice is, of course, laudable as long as it is planned with intelligence and placed within an appropriate and relevant context. When the area under discussion is customer related, such as service delivery, that context has to be customers and their profitability, both actual and potential. That requires knowing as much as possible about those customers and their relationship with, and perceptions of, the supplier. It requires an understanding of customer profitability and its drivers; and it means making difficult trade-offs between 'best practice' and what is commercially sensible. Gaining these insights is hard enough for the business whose customers are under examination. For an outside firm to achieve the same degree of understanding as part of a best practice or benchmarking study is a tough task indeed.

INCENTIVIZING INAPPROPRIATE BEHAVIOUR

Recent years have seen a growing transfer of practices from the commercial world to manage and improve the quality of delivery within the public services. The health and education sectors come particularly to mind. Targets are set for hospital waiting times. League tables of school performance are published in which exam results are the primary measure for determining a school's position on the ladder. Directly or indirectly, the pay and career progression of staff come to depend, at least in part, on achieving the desired outcomes. Small wonder then that the media are increasingly dominated by stories of casualty trolleys in corridors being designated as hospital beds to reduce reported waiting times, and of schools managing their exam-entrance criteria to achieve the best possible pass rates. The targets may be met, but the true objectives will not.

Sometimes such manipulation is a complete flouting of agreed rules; more often, it is simply playing the game, just not in the way intended. Always, it is dysfunctional. The objective has shifted from the laudable (improving health care and educational standards) to the flawed but understandable (keeping one's job and achieving career progression).

A similar pattern can be seen in many customer communications and service-delivery operations. Senior management frequently espouses the need to deliver the highest-quality service to customers and then measures and rewards call centre staff on the volume of calls answered, with no attempt to assess their quality, or the levels of profitability and customer satisfaction generated by the repeat business.

One senior manager of a large financial services business took understanding the customer experience and focusing on their needs extremely seriously. He regularly went 'back to the floor' to see what was actually happening, at first hand. On one occasion, he visited a very busy call centre and took the opportunity to listen in. Three calls in particular captured his attention. In every case, the customers were frustrated and complaining. In every case, the operators dealt with the customer quickly, courteously and efficiently. In every case, the problem could not be solved immediately which, unwittingly, further increased client dissatisfaction.

The MIS reported that all calls were answered within three rings, no call lasted more than two and a half minutes, operators had acceptable levels of down-time and no calls were abandoned. It was a very successful day and, if repeated throughout the year, call-centre bonuses would reflect the achievement of the agreed service measures. However, in all three cases (and by inference probably many more) customers were in reality dissatisfied and unhappy. The MIS did not measure that, or the likelihood and cost of their subsequent defection.

Had call-centre systems been capable of indicating client value, the operators would have been allowed more time to handle calls from profitable customers, and the company would have been able to track just how many of its high-value clients used the service – and with what results. It would also have had the information to assess the viability of differentiated service levels.

A life assurance company that operated a large call centre employed two different types of staff. The bulk of the operators (the customer assistants) were trained to be able to describe the features of the products the company sold, leaving the decision about what and whether to buy to the customer. The regulations (legislative and internal) precluded them from offering advice on a customer's individual circumstances. To cater for those customers who wanted more than merely information or had complex needs, there was a second, smaller team that was qualified and authorized to give advice.

The profitability of the advice team was under intense scrutiny. Their productivity was low. Very few customers seemed to need the expensive skills that the team possessed. Disbanding the operation was a real possibility.

After a short investigation, it was soon clear that, contrary to the management team's perceived wisdom, there were in fact very many customers who, if they were referred to the advice team, would not only benefit from the advice given but would also do business at much higher levels than was otherwise the case. So where were these customers hiding? Why weren't they being referred?

They were, in fact, there all the time. But the team that took the initial call – the customer assistants – were remunerated on the basis of their own sales performance. If they passed on a call, they received only limited credit for any subsequent sale. Also, sales that arose from the intervention of the advisers were more complex and took much longer to process. The net result was that the customer assistants were trying to close the sales themselves, albeit at much lower values. This dysfunctional behaviour arose directly from the introduction of a dysfunctional reward system.

Misaligning Objectives and Strategy

Failing to keep strategy in line with objectives happens all too often where the planning process occurs in isolation from the everyday running of the business, or where the strategy and objectives are regarded as the domain of the Board, rather than a business activity that involves *everyone* in the organization.

When a financial services institution (FSI) establishes a goal to become the 'provider of choice' in its sector and dedicates itself to the highest possible standards of customer care, it can come as a shock when the same institution is required to pay a substantial fine to the Financial Services Authority for mis-selling investment products. Yet this has happened all too frequently: not because senior management deliberately set out to be duplicitous, but because the objectives and strategy of the company were not adequately translated into the ways in which the business actually operated on a day-to-day basis.

The sales managers within many FSIs were given significant financial incentives to grow their teams. As long as potential recruits had the necessary regulatory approval, they were hired. Their employment contracts and remuneration packages were designed so that, while there were real costs to the business for induction and training, the immediate cash downside of unsuitable recruits was acceptable.

Once new sales people were out in the field, if they didn't generate new business they simply faded away, usually leaving of their own accord as their earnings dwindled. On the other hand, If they were productive they received plaudits, recognition and significant levels of remuneration. The existence of complex regulatory paperwork designed to validate the appropriateness of their sales proved largely irrelevant. These were clever people with huge monetary incentives to manipulate the system. They were managed by people who also had a strong financial motivation to 'do the business' – and who knew just how far to push their luck.

This lack of connection between the company's stated goals and strategy and the reality in the field was almost certain to end in tears. It has, for far too many firms.

The Shift from Inappropriate to Illegal Behaviour

The ingenuity and skill of sales people in exploiting the system (particularly when given the right incentive and a lack of controls) can sometimes become more than merely dysfunctional. A pensions company, which rewarded sales staff on the basis of each new policy, discovered that one of its people had been paid commissions over a two-year period for sales that had never taken place. This crafty (if criminal) individual discovered that if a new case was submitted for an existing customer (but not a new customer) he would receive his commission before the case was actually put on the books. What is more, there was no mechanism in place for him to repay it. So he simply extracted customer records from the files, filled in applications ostensibly for these people (a process the customer knew nothing about) and ensured that the paperwork contained one or more errors. This meant that, rather than being processed in the usual way resulting in customers discovering that they had 'bought' a pension they hadn't asked for, the case was referred back to the sales person, who then conveniently lost the paperwork. This 'nice little earner' only came to light when a more than usually helpful customer service clerk, instead of simply returning the faulty paperwork to the sales person, contacted the customer to see if she could sort out the problem directly. The result was predictably terminal for the sales person concerned.

TECHNOLOGY TURMOIL

There can be little doubt that the most skilled and persuasive sales people are to be found in the technology arena. How else can we explain the never-ending saga of failed, and failing, technology projects – in both the private and public sectors – accompanied by the continued success of the vendors? It can be argued that since world equity markets started falling in 2000 such success is more muted, but this phenomenon does not change the general proposition.

The Triumph of Salesmanship

The continued triumph of salesmanship over reality can be seen with particular clarity in the customer-service arena. It is now about 20 years since companies started to spend significant sums on technology-led solutions to the challenge of managing customers and achieving greater customer focus. This began with the creation of customer databases and so-called data warehouses, to allow firms to identify and manage the entirety of their relationships with individual customers. Telephony technology emerged with the ability to feed pre-dialled outgoing calls to customer-service staff and route inbound calls via menus and voice-recognition systems. Next came the development of innovative analytical tools like neural networks to build models that could predict customer behaviour. This was closely followed by the phenomenal rise of Customer Relationship Marketing (CRM) technologies that brought together and enhanced the previous, typically stand-alone, initiatives.

Hundreds of millions of pounds have been spent in the UK alone, by hundreds of companies. For the majority, the results have been largely illusory. Little real benefit has been achieved. Customer lifetime values have hardly changed, the rate of cross-selling to existing customers is little different and customers still view most organizations with at best indifference and at worst resentment. So hats off to the technology sales people!

Why has so little been achieved? The technology (much of it anyway) is fundamentally sound. The people implementing it are bright and capable. The potential for improvement most surely exists.

The answers are complex, but at their heart lies a key issue. Most technology implementations begin with fundamentally flawed objectives. Objectives such as reducing headcount, improving process efficiency and enhancing the customer experience are not truly objectives, they are consequences. The real objectives should be customer focused and revenue related. Even when the over-riding issue facing a business is to reduce costs, and the chosen strategy for doing so is through the introduction of technology, the absence of a customer-focused approach will more often than not lead to disaster unless there is a commercially proven case for the technology purchase.

An Investment House Example

In the mid-1990s, one of the UK's largest investment houses rec-ognized that the world in which it competed was going to change radically and its historically very attractive margins were going to come under increasing pressure, both from new competitors and regulatory legislation. A large team was assembled to redesign and rebuild the business with a significantly reduced cost base. Progress was rapid and impressive. Redundant processes were eliminated, operations were streamlined, premises were rational-ized. The innovative use of technology was, naturally, a significant element in much of the change.

At one point, someone examined the nature of the inbound tele-phone calls being received in the various customer-service centres. This analysis showed that the largest single source of calls (nearly 50 per cent of the total) was from investors seeking an up-to-date valuation of a single fund, or of their entire portfolio. As a result of work done elsewhere, all customers had been assigned unique identification and security numbers. Also, the funds-management database had been rationalized to produce a single apparent data source that could be interrogated by other systems within the busi-ness. Putting these together, the project team decided to investigate how costs could be further reduced by using automated telephone-response technology. In the plan that emerged, customers would be given a dedicated line for valuations, or transferred to that line from the menu of options provided by the general customer-service number. By responding to a simple (well, fairly simple) set of menu options and keying in their customer and security numbers, customers would be able to secure an up-to-date valuation without a single human ever being involved. The potential cost savings were immense.

It was then that someone asked a simple question: 'Why do customers ask for valuations?' Rather disturbingly, no one seemed to know for sure. Two quick pieces of work were done. First, arrangements were made to listen to a cross-section of customers' valuation-request calls. Second, those customers' account details were tracked over the weeks following their initial call.

The work was far from perfect. The sample of customers monitored was probably not random, as not all customers could be followed due to systems limitations and the tracking only continued for a short time. Nevertheless, a clear pattern emerged. A significant proportion of callers was asking for a valuation immediately prior to closing their account or selling a particular holding. But if their call was handled by a senior customer-service representative and at a time when the service centre was relatively quiet, the customer would frequently remain active, staying with their existing funds or sometimes switching to another of the company's products.

By taking the customer-service staff out of the loop, it was apparent that automating the valuations process would lead to a very significant loss of customer revenue and profit, far outweighing the potential cost savings. Indeed, a back-of-an-envelope calculation suggested that increasing the number of qualified staff in the call centre would keep business that might otherwise be lost, at a very attractive return on investment.

Technology can transform business operations. It can reduce operating costs and allow customers to be communicated with, and managed, in ways that were unimaginable just a few years ago. But it is not an end in itself. It rarely, if ever, conveys lasting competitive advantage as the newest solutions are almost always available to anyone with deep enough pockets, or the sense to employ consultants who have implemented them before for competitors. Technology is (or should be) simply an enabler and facilitator of a strategy that more efficiently and profitably meets customer needs.

EVERYONE EMBRACES CHANGE ENTHUSIASTICALLY

Believe the above statement if you will, but in most companies the majority of people are fearful of change. They just do not admit it. Of course, there are some who thrive on it and grasp the opportunities that it brings. If you are very lucky, or have managed to build balanced teams across the business, these people will be spread throughout the organization in sufficient numbers to make change happen relatively easily and profitably.

Most successful senior managers approach change positively and with enthusiasm, which is one of the key reasons they have reached their current position. However, sometimes their acceptance of the need for change can be divorced from the rest of the business. When change is needed, they have to rely on pressure from the top to force the pace. If a company seeks to innovate across all its areas of activity, that single point of momentum can often prove inadequate. When only those parts of the business that are readily visible to senior management really embrace the desired change, pockets of resistance and traditionalism will remain.

As has been said repeatedly, for customer focus to deliver improved value for shareholders, it has to be a company-wide activity. Given the scale and breadth of change required, a planned and methodical approach to managing it is almost always essential.

An Assembly of Individuals

To describe change within large businesses, many commentators use the metaphor of steering a giant supertanker at sea. The sheer scale and momentum of the vessel require significant time for any alteration in course to be effected. But the metaphor is flawed, because any organization, however large, is actually an assembly of individuals, not a single and solid entity. Perhaps a better image is of a large number of people paddling canoes. Survival demands that they all paddle in roughly the same direction and at roughly the same speed. Unlike the supertanker, though, they do have the ability to change course with great speed. All that is needed is that each individual has enough space, they all understand what change of direction is required, and they all have the necessary motivation to follow the course, roughly simultaneously.

Most customer-oriented change programmes focus, not unreasonably, on the mechanics: on the interlinking of deliverables, the coordination of work streams and the critical events that need to take place to effect successful transformation. In all too many businesses, insufficient attention is paid to the human consequences. To achieve customer focus, it is essential to have the commitment and support of the whole organization.

Creating organizations that have the ability to evolve rapidly and embrace new horizons is not the subject of this book. Nevertheless, some reference is necessary to how the people within an organization should be involved, motivated and aligned with the required change. Figure 7.1 summarizes one proven approach.

This model illustrates the key elements: communication, selling the vision, gaining commitment, providing support and transition management. These are mapped against the three phases that typically occur when most people are challenged by the prospect of the new.

The Ending

In this phase it first becomes apparent that the status quo is about to change. Perhaps the most frequent reason for resistance is that staff only become involved when all the important analyses and decisions have been taken and they are faced with a *fait accompli*. Even worse is the situation where people become aware that change is afoot through unofficial, uncontrolled communications, often in the form of gossip and rumour. Of course, no business can be managed profitably by having everyone involved in every decision and often the changes needed may represent a real threat to some people's careers. But communicating early will set the foundations for a successful programme and avoid the rumour mill that will quickly, and destructively, fill the void if official communication is not forthcoming.

The Bridging

This phase is often ignored. Once the challenges created by the threat of imminent change (the *ending*) have been overcome,

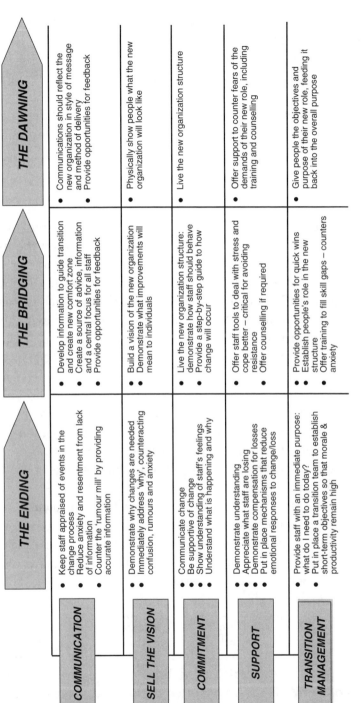

Figure 7.1 Managing customer-focused change
Reproduced with permission of Valoris Ltd

managers often assume that all that remains is to implement the new approach. In fact, for a great number of people the period following the announcement of change can prove to be a very emotionally trying time. Many organizations witness significant increases in sickness and absenteeism. More worryingly, this is often the time when internecine fighting breaks out and the rate of progress towards a new business model slows, or is even halted entirely.

The Dawning

A well-managed and communicated change programme will eventually bring people to the final phase, the *dawning*, when the new order is accepted and embraced. The more dynamic and persuasive the senior management team has been in promoting innovation, the greater the need for a rigorous change-management approach. This paradox is often overlooked by senior managers, whose personal attitudes to the challenge are likely to be distant from the majority of staff. The differences in attitudes across the organization are almost always dangerously significant. The perception is often that it is only the 'ordinary workers' who suffer adverse consequences and that senior management are almost always able to protect themselves. This is increasingly not the case, but it is perception that drives behaviour. A considered and organized approach to both the procedural and human aspects of change is an obvious requirement.

The profound benefits that can accrue from adopting a customer-focused strategy can be lost if the people in the business who meet, talk and write to customers have not understood the purpose behind the new approach, or fail to be convinced that new ways of working are of benefit to all concerned.

Every point of contact with the customer is an opportunity: to reinforce the customer's view that choosing to do business with you was sound; or to strengthen the already hardening belief that this is a rotten company with which to do business. Unless the move towards a customer-focused business can embrace these 'moments of truth', as they have often been called, its benefits will be at best limited and at worst invisible.

REORGANIZING FOR FOCUS

Isn't reorganization wonderful? How we all enjoy the disruption, confusion, loss of productivity and general chaos that ensues whenever a major reorganization of roles and responsibilities comes along. There are few large firms in the UK that have not experienced these joys in recent years, either resulting from mergers and acquisitions or from the ministrations of consultants. Where once, not so many years ago, it seemed that many senior managers regarded regular and profound reorganization as a means of enlivening and reinvigorating the business, the frequency of change has, perhaps inevitably, now resulted in reorganization fatigue and disillusionment.

After presiding over a series of acquisitions that trebled his business revenues and involved the integration of four major operating units, the chief executive of one of the UK's largest service companies decided, not unreasonably perhaps, that his staff had had enough of reorganization. Faced with a fairly major challenge in one of his markets, his consultancy brief stated: 'I'll consider any solution, but I don't want changes to the organization chart anywhere in the business.'

Reorganizing: A Means to An End

It is profoundly damaging to a business to regard reorganization as an end in itself, as many seem to believe. Similarly, many managers seek tidiness and elegance in organizational design, ahead of pragmatism and stability. Conversely, a refusal to consider reorganization as an option can severely affect the degree to which a business is truly able to focus on its customers. The approaches to and philosophy of customer focus have an impact on the entire business. No part of the organization can be exempt from the changes in attitudes and working practices that are required.

In tackling the issues raised by the pursuit of customer focus, many challenges to conventional organizational thinking will emerge. Prescriptive solutions are pointless. Each firm embarking on the journey has to resolve its own, specific organizational challenges in the light of its own particular competitive,

environmental and financial situation, and the attitudes, perceptions and profitability of its customers. The flexibility and open-
mindedness of the senior team are key determinants of success.

This book proposes no specific organizational solutions. These
can only be crafted on a case-by-case basis. Nevertheless, it is
important to identify some of the most intractable challenges that
will emerge and discuss how they might be tackled.

Business Unit Battlefields

The concept of the discrete business unit, often referred to as a
strategic business unit (SBU), with its own profit and loss account
and management team, has been a tremendous boon for many
large companies that previously failed to achieve the level of organizational dynamism and energy required. Relatively small units
(which can still be large businesses), tasked with clear goals and
accountabilities and with rewards closely linked to performance,
have proved a winning formula, but there can still be problems.

One of the world's leading international airlines owns a holiday
company subsidiary that is a separate SBU to its core travel business. The travel operation will not (and probably cannot because
its systems will not allow it) make changes to tickets issued by the
holiday company. From the customer's perspective this is a very
strange state of affairs. The corporate ownership is the same, the
branding is the same, and the distinction between holidays and
travel is a semantic nicety that will escape almost everyone. The
lack of a 'joined-up business' becomes merely a source of irritation
that increases the probability of customers looking elsewhere next
time they are planning a trip.

In practice, joining up SBUs is not easy. The strength of the
concept flows in no small part from the freedom and independence
given to managers. The more absolutely and relatively successful
those managers are, the more they will tend to protect their own
empire against the rest of the organization.

This can become a major issue, particularly when the performance of one SBU outstrips the others. A large UK bank organized
itself into SBUs, one of which was responsible for credit cards. This
very profitable and, by any measure, successful operation became

more and more estranged from the organization as a whole. An outside observer would have thought that the businesses were unconnected if it were not for the bank's name on the cards. Few if any companies can withstand the trauma and disruption of this type of behaviour. The bank in question was no exception; it eventually fired its chief executive and lost its independence to a smaller competitor.

Who Owns the Customer?

The very use of the words 'customer ownership' should set alarm bells ringing. The fact is that no company, division or product group ever 'owns' a customer; to use the word implies a fundamental lack of understanding about the nature of customers, whether they are consumers or businesses.

Yet one of the most frequent debates in all companies organized around product groups concerns who owns the customer. Many businesses, such as the bank referred to above, organize themselves around products. This approach has many benefits. It brings together technical expertise with an ability to understand the market and the competition, and often allows a comparatively simple organizational structure to emerge. Where the product defines the customer group, which was not the case with the bank, it can work extremely well; but in a business where customers buy from across a product range, complications can often arise. If product group A has acquired and 'owns' a customer, on what basis should product group B be granted access to that customer?

Customers are an asset of the business as a whole. That asset has to be managed to maximize the long-term return on its acquisition and management cost. Doing this requires the company to take the broadest possible view of the customer and put forward the most relevant propositions, at the most relevant times, driven only by the need to maximize long-term returns on the often hidden asset that is the customer – *that* is customer focus.

To imagine that a customer is ever owned reveals a mindset that ignores the realities of a commercial world in which the choice of suppliers in most industries is huge and frequently growing. Worse still, it fails to understand the way in which customers think. It is akin to the same sloppy thinking that leads people into the trap of talking about building customer relationships.

Except for a small number of mainly (but not exclusively) business-to-business sectors, the word 'relationship' and its implication of reciprocity are entirely misplaced. Companies may think they want a relationship with their customers but, in the vast majority of cases, it is a sure bet that their customers do not want one with them.

Customers are not owned, ever. At best, a company can lease a small part of its customers' attention. The terms of the lease are in the customers' favour. They can ignore you, forget you or desert you at the time of their choosing, without giving reasons or notice – and without any right of appeal.

Not so Normal Distribution

When products, or product groups, are not chosen as the basis for an organization's structure, the alternative is often to select distribution channels. This can, and frequently does, produce a quite remarkable degree of parochialism. Now, as well as the self-interest of the channel managers, there are the demands and interests of distribution partners and intermediaries.

A large pensions company told one of its policy holders that it could not deal with his enquiry directly, even though it had a sales force and customer-service teams of its own, as he had to go through the intermediary who sold him the policy. The customer explained that it was 20 years since he took out the pension, he had not spoken to the intermediary since and, indeed, could not remember the person concerned. In any case, he now lived in France and not the UK, where the pension was originally taken out. Undaunted by this, the champions of the channel helpfully, but misguidedly, suggested that they could find the address of the intermediary concerned for him.

Incidentally, it perhaps says something about the customer focus of the life assurance and pensions industry that the standard industry terminology for a customer of an intermediary who no longer operates for the company is an 'orphan'. The connotations of a customer who is unloved, a potential problem and for whom no one really wishes to take responsibility are all too apt in far too many cases.

Most successful managers seek to build simple organizations in which responsibilities are clear. That way, the team can be set unambiguous individual objectives and measured, and rewarded, against predetermined criteria. Taking a customer-focused view can make that ideal harder to achieve. Many different managerial approaches exist, from matrix management to the creation of high-level customer-management functions spanning products and distribution. None is fundamentally flawed, but all will fail if the management team does not share a common vision of the customer as the ultimate source of commercial wealth generation.

CHANGING A LIGHT BULB

How many psychiatrists does it take to change a light bulb? Only one, but the light bulb must really want to change.

Transforming a business into one that is really focused on its customers is rather like that. Good intentions, fine words and even lots of effort and investment will achieve little if the organization lacks the inner will to make the necessary transformation.

What are the steps towards customer focus? How should the task be managed, planned and implemented? What are the common mistakes and pitfalls? How can you put your ideas into an actionable plan that balances customer orientation with commercial gain? Such an action plan is the subject of the next chapter.

Chapter 8

Bringing the Focus Alive
A Practical Action Plan

There are risks and costs to a program of action. But they are far less than the long-range risks and costs of comfortable inaction.

J F Kennedy, 12 May 1961

The managing director of a major division of a large UK financial services business was absolutely convinced that his business, and its various divisions, needed to become far more customer focused. So convinced was he that he convened a project team, led by the head of IT, and briefed them to find, hire and manage a reputable firm of consultants to make it all happen.

The consulting brief was written and several firms were requested to tender for the work. However, the need was urgent, so the deadline for the submission of proposals was only one week. The project was new, the team members were very busy and the potential scope of the assistance required was vast and diverse. It was therefore difficult for the tendering organizations really to understand the scope and nature of the work, and exactly what it was the organization wanted to achieve.

The various consulting firms adopted a range of different approaches. Some argued that the company must decide its customer-management strategy before implementing any new technological solutions and adopting new processes or practices. Others made the case for the introduction of the latest CRM technology as a matter of urgency, on the principle that it had all the functionality the bank would ever need. How it was to be used once integrated and tested could be decided as the work proceeded. The latter argument prevailed and the proposing organization, a very large and respected management consultancy, was hired to develop the appropriate solutions.

It soon became apparent, however, that the work would be far more complex than envisaged. The consultants, quite naturally, asked the project managers about their objectives for the technology, so that it might be configured to meet the company's needs. They enquired about the developmental priorities so that they could address the most important issues first. They asked how the technology would be managed, how it was to be used by the various sub-divisions, and how the resulting customer-management programmes would be measured for their success.

The project team could only use their best judgement and their not inconsiderable experience to answer these thorny issues because divisional managers had not been invited to join the team and, in any case, they were extremely busy running their own business units. Not surprisingly, this resulted in a degree of over-engineering so as to cope with all eventualities, on the principle that it was better to build in the greatest possible flexibility to cater for known, and currently unknown, future needs. The scope and cost of the project escalated. What was supposed to take less than one year took the better part of two, but the technology was finally implemented and everyone was happy. Well, the consultants were happy with their fees. The project team was happy that it was all over. Senior managers were happy that they now had a state-of-the-art technological solution.

The managing director announced the new order and urged his direct reports to develop appropriate plans to take advantage of the investment. It quickly became apparent that none of the sub-divisions actually wanted the technology, regarding it as a sledge-hammer to crack a nut. It was unwieldy and believed to be unnecessary for the number and types of customers they served.

Nearly three years since the project was first conceived, the company is no nearer to realizing the greater customer focus that it sought. It has, however, spent a great deal of money, consumed a vast amount of management time and managed to spawn many inter-divisional arguments. Could there have been a better approach and what can be learned from this unfortunate episode?

AN ACTION PLAN FOR CUSTOMER FOCUS

As with all things, there can be no single approach that is valid for every company and every situation. The work programme required will be different in every case. However, there are a number of relatively straightforward principles illustrated in Figure 8.1 and discussed in detail in the paragraphs that follow.

MANAGING THE CUSTOMER FOCUS PROCESS

How should a process of such potential complexity, importance and cost be managed?

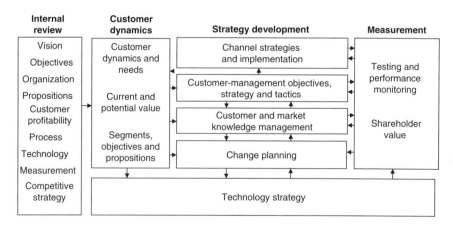

Figure 8.1   A customer focus action plan
Reproduced and adapted with permission of the Virtual Partnership Ltd

Don't Call it a Project

Creating customer focus is about radical, and lasting, change to an organization, the way it operates and the way it thinks. Projects, on the other hand, have a beginning, a middle and an end.

Make the Chief Executive the Programme Sponsor

Let it be known that the chief executive is fully supportive of the initiative. Make the programme a regular board agenda item and expect those involved to report regularly on their progress and the issues they have encountered.

Set Realistic and Achievable Milestones and Deliverables

Measure progress rigorously. Establish a realistic budget, for both development and testing. Include not only the costs of testing the technology, systems and processes, but also the resulting customer communications or interactions. Very few things in life work perfectly first time. Profiting from customer focus is an iterative and ongoing process that is never complete. It is therefore critical to foster a culture whereby sensible developmental testing is lauded and any failure is regarded as a learning experience.

Establish Cross-Functional Teams

Staff the development teams with people from different parts of the organization and at varying levels. Enlist a mix of iconoclasts and pragmatic business managers to create the necessary balance. Challenge them to think like customers, but behave like accountants.

Use an 'Impartial' Manager to Lead the Charge

Quite obviously, everyone has a business speciality; however, avoid using a manager who is blinkered or has a particular axe to grind. The marketing director may be the best qualified, but only if she will be receptive to financial arguments. The IT director may understand the technological implications, but will he fully appreciate the marketing and sales issues? The chief financial officer will manage costs and needs to be committed to the customer-profitability calculations, but will she understand the challenges of multichannel distribution, for example? The key is to achieve the widest possible breadth of experience, combined with an open mind and the authority, and inclination, to challenge the status quo.

Use External Consultants Judiciously

While consultants are frequently vilified, the right companies do have the advantage of experience. For many within any organization, addressing a challenge of this magnitude will be a once-in-a-lifetime event. Appropriately qualified consultants will have worked with a wide variety of different companies, will have encountered many of the problems before, and may have the experience and process-management skills that will add value. Listen to their advice, but do not follow it slavishly. They have a business model that is probably very different to yours.

Communicate Frequently

Communicate to report progress, establish commitment and disseminate results. Regular communications from senior management establish and cement the commercial imperative. Advertising positive results motivates and galvanizes the entire organization. Bad news, if positioned as a learning experience, encourages creativity and innovation – as long as the actions were apparently sensible at the outset. Appreciate that different people react to change in different ways and at different speeds.

Recognize that the Planning Will Be Iterative

The work will never be finished. The strategy selected will influence the processes needed and the technologies chosen. Similarly, as technology changes the art of the possible, so it will affect the strategy and the processes needed to support it. Striving for customer focus is a never-ending task because customers' needs constantly evolve as competitors raise expectations, technology evolves and the economic and social environments change.

THE INTERNAL REVIEW

Whatever the developmental process adopted, the starting point must always be an appraisal of where the organization is now, whether this is called an internal review or, perhaps rather more emotively, an audit. Where exactly is the company situated in terms of the ways in which it currently manages its customers? What are its capabilities and resources? What are its strengths and where are its weaknesses? Only by truly understanding the current state can the practicality and affordability of any new order be assessed. Furthermore, unless the current situation is described and documented, it will be extremely difficult (if not impossible) to compare and contrast new ways of working with what went before and, hence, understand whether what has been changed represents a real improvement.

The areas of investigation should include at least the following.

Vision

Does the organization have a single, shared and comprehensible customer-focused vision? Is there a common understanding about what will be altered when greater customer focus is achieved? How will the company behave differently towards its customers; and how will customers behave differently in terms of what they buy, or how frequently, or at what average transaction values? People often struggle to express a vision without resorting to clichés or platitudes. One way to tackle this challenge is to invite them to describe what it will feel like to be a customer under the new order. Once this has been done, the other elements of vision may be easier to articulate. Without a clear indication of direction, any path is as good as every other.

Objectives

Do company objectives exist for the management of customers? If so, do such objectives relate to their current, or future, levels of profitability? Do they specify how they want customers to behave in the future in order to improve sales and profits? Do any of them relate to how it will feel as a customer in the new order?

Organization

Does the company have the mindset and is it organized in such a way as to achieve customer focus? Have customers been segmented into meaningful and actionable groups? Is the business structured around product lines, customer groups or segments? Is there an ethos of continuous testing and measurement? Are the ways in which customers are managed reviewed and improved regularly, based on internal and external stimuli, in order to improve their effectiveness or profitability?

Propositions

Are the customer propositions compelling and profitable, and do they reinforce the strategy of the company as a whole? Are they regularly tested and improved? Are they 'one size fits all' or do they recognize the discrete needs of specific customer segments? Are systems, processes and training in place to deliver the propositions seamlessly and cost-effectively, by all staff and through all channels?

Customer Profitability

Are customer profitability and potential calculated? Are all activities aligned to increase these values through tried-and-tested means of up-selling, cross-selling and retention? Are products and services offered to customers in the way(s) they prefer, at the times they need them, through channels of their preference, as far as it is profitable to do so? Do customer communications recognize customer value and their purchase life stage?

Processes

Is the current customer-management strategy implemented across all channels and through all campaigns? Are interactions based on high-quality and consistent customer analysis and information? Do clearly defined processes exist for managing customers, or segments, throughout their lifetime with the company, from prospect to lapsed customer to reactivated customer?

Technology

Are customer-facing staffs supported by technologies that provide timely information and prompts? Do systems enable all staff to manage customer dialogue intelligently at the point of contact or sale and maximize the value of the relationship? Do systems specify appropriate sales or servicing actions to take with an individual customer or prospect, based on segment and purchase-propensity information and/or potential value enhancement? Do staff have access to all relevant customer information and the status of the customer's current relationship with, and value to, the company?

Measurement

Are responsibilities and accountabilities for the maintenance and development of a customer knowledge-management system and strategy defined? Are customer-performance metrics specified and tracked to promote a customer-focused approach? Is reporting automated and designed to support key decision making? Do processes and procedures exist to share customer-related data throughout the organization? Are customer complaints and satisfaction levels monitored across all customer contact points, on an ongoing basis; and are they used as inputs into continuous process improvement?

The list is potentially almost endless, but all aspects of the review process should be designed around the resolution of two key issues. First, does the organization understand and learn from its customers; second, does it satisfy their needs seamlessly, profitably and in ways that reinforce the company's chosen competitive strategy?

CUSTOMER DYNAMICS AND NEEDS

Once the scope of the challenge has been identified it is, of course, necessary to decide what to do to manage customers more profitably in the future. No doubt, during the review many ideas will have come to mind. Some will make sound commercial common sense. By rectifying glaring errors or taking advantage of previously missed opportunities, 'quick wins' can often be achieved. Acting on the blindingly obvious should not be delayed and can frequently help galvanize the organization by providing some immediate financial payback and positively reinforcing the fact that things are actually changing.

One large home shopping company undertaking such a review identified extremely poor response levels from its attempts to sell further merchandise with the customers' first product delivery. This seemed nonsensical to all concerned until the credit controller announced that in fact demand from this source was very high, but that his department was sensibly rejecting all the orders because the customers' creditworthiness had yet to be established. At a stroke, the objective for the communication was changed from an overt attempt to sell to one soliciting payment for the goods received, on the principle that the faster a valid credit history could be established, the faster additional cross-sales could be effected.

Do not allow the desire for quick wins to divert attention from the ultimate prize. The urge to plug *all* the gaps should be resisted until a greater knowledge of customers, their needs and values has been established. As has been said repeatedly, not all customers are the same, nor do they have the same needs or value. Attempting to manage all customers as if they were a homogeneous group can lead to some very wrong-headed thinking, simply because strategies will be developed for the average customer – and the average customer only exists because of the inadequacies of our current systems, thinking and measurement capabilities. For every 'average' banking customer who has bought just one additional product from their current account supplier, there are many who have bought four or five and an even greater number who have bought none at all. Although the average UK debit-card transaction value is around £35, some people use their card to buy their annual family holiday, while many others are simply buying a new pair of socks.

Value-Based Customer Segmentation

The next step in the journey must therefore be to develop the greater customer understanding required to manage each group as profitably as possible. Value-based customer segmentation is critical. Who are the frequent, high-value purchasers? Who are the low-value testers? Which customers offer the greatest potential for further growth and development and which should be targeted for disinvestment? What do the behaviour patterns and purchase life-cycles of such customers look like and how do they differ from each other? The key task at this stage is to differentiate, in a meaningful way, between discrete customer groups so that appropriate growth and development objectives can be set and an affordable level of investment calculated for each.

Customer Research

Questions relating to value and purchase behaviour can only be answered through detailed and insightful data analysis. Only by studying how much customers actually spend and how they actually behave can an accurate picture be developed. True customer focus demands that the organization *knows* its customers on an individual level but *manages* them according to their current and future profitability, tempered by an in-depth understanding of their needs and preferences. While customer research has an invaluable role to play in understanding the characteristics, needs and motivations of the various data-driven customer groups, it can be a poor and potentially misleading tool if it is used to define the segments themselves.

Customer research does, however, have a very important role to play. It can help answer why customers behave as they do and, therefore, whether there is anything the organization can do to improve their profitability. Some shoppers are very brand loyal, while others buy for reasons of convenience or from a range of suppliers because they value variety. Some buy frequently because they have a preferred source, others are simply heavy users and buy from many different suppliers. Research can help to identify these, and other, characteristics that enable the right objectives to be set in recognition of each segment's particular behaviour patterns. It can assist in distinguishing between customers that appear to have the same value, but may have very different potential and thereby demand very different messages and propositions if their profitability is to be maximized.

SEGMENT OBJECTIVES AND PROPOSITIONS

Once the customer segments have been identified, it is necessary to specify the objectives and proposition, or range of propositions, for each. It is at this stage that matters so often go spectacularly wrong.

How many large business-to-consumer companies are there, for example, that organize themselves into two separate teams for customer acquisition and retention? The task of the acquisition team is typically to bring customers through the door, in the greatest numbers and at the lowest cost possible. Do they care about the subsequent behaviour and profitability of the customers they have acquired? Of course not. They are measured and rewarded for volume. The retention team, on the other hand, is charged with the responsibility for keeping these expensively inherited recruits and maintaining the largest possible customer base.

In companies that cannot calculate and monitor customer profitability, the result is chaos and inefficiency. The acquirers will consistently look for new and innovative ways to keep the front-end numbers high and the sales costs low. No matter that they might use short-term propositions, such as gifts or price incentives, which may actively encourage and condition customer promiscuity – it is simply not their problem. In addition, the retention managers will use all the tools at their disposal to keep the customers actively buying, regardless of their profitability. Unsurprisingly, they will squander money on customers who have little, if any, potential value, and do practically anything to avoid them lapsing or defecting – despite the fact that the company's overall profitably may be enhanced immeasurably by allowing them to do so. The result is a customer-management madhouse that is a continual drain on shareholder value.

The same is true in many business-to-business organizations. Here the sales force is tasked with winning new business, while the account managers flog the dead horses. And it is not always the small accounts that are the least profitable. Research and personal experience have proven time and again that it is frequently the larger accounts that can be the least profitable. Large accounts frequently expect the highest and most expensive servicing, typically have more transactions, require more expensive and frequent face-to-face interaction and demand the lowest prices.

The Return on Customer Investment

These avoidable situations, which occur all too frequently, arise primarily because someone, somewhere set the wrong objectives. The simplistic beliefs that gaining new customers is 'good' and losing them is 'bad' are wrong-headed and expensive. It would be far better for businesses to set targets based on the return on customer investment, as most organizations do for all other asset acquisitions, even when they cost a fraction of the price.

Under such a model, the costs of customer acquisition, servicing and retention are amalgamated and forecast over the customer's purchase lifetime, with a calculation of net present value thrown in. The objective for customer management thereafter is then simply to maximize the return on this expenditure. When considered in isolation, it truly does not matter whether it costs a lot to acquire a new customer and it is largely irrelevant that some customers consume more resources than others. What should be of concern is the economics of the whole relationship. If expensive customers also produce the most value, then the investment will probably have been worthwhile. If cheap customers depress profits, the investment in them must be decreased until the return again becomes acceptable.

Setting Segment Objectives

Spending time on setting the right customer-segment objectives is critical. How often have you seen proposals for work programmes that specify 10 (or more) different objectives? In seeking to achieve greater customer focus, the objectives frequently relate to keeping customers longer; to making them feel warmer about the organization; to increasing the company's share of their wallet; to reducing the costs of retention; to maximizing cross-sales and up-sales; or to servicing them through the channels of their choice. All are laudable, but not one of them comprises the *real* objective for wanting to become more customer focused, which is, of course, to make more money and produce greater shareholder value.

The Fit with Business Strategy

It follows that there must be an unambiguous fit between a company's objectives, its chosen business strategy and the propositions that it puts before its customers. British Airways obviously decided that, despite the growth in discount air travel, its strategy to serve high-value business customers was incompatible with a cut-price, no-frills servicing policy, which is arguably why it launched Go. In contrast, easyJet built its business on the premise that it would be the lowest-cost operator and its customer proposition is perfectly aligned: lowest costs, lowest fares.

Marks & Spencer was reported to have suffered badly because its fashion range selections were at odds with the needs of its customers. In reality, the situation was probably more serious than a few merchandise buying errors, which may be one of the reasons that it has taken so long for the company to recover. The store was built on a customer proposition based around high-quality, value-for-money products, primarily clothing, aimed at consumers who were perhaps not as fashion conscious as others. M&S was trusted to deliver and arguably it lost that trust. Its in-store proposition became out of kilter with its avowed business strategy – and it was punished at the tills accordingly.

CUSTOMER-MANAGEMENT OBJECTIVES, STRATEGY AND TACTICS

Now that the high-level, preparatory work has been done, it is time to embark on the hard work. All of the activities described previously are of course essential, but none specifies what you should actually do, when you should do it and at whom it should be directed. The starting point must be an understanding of the key business drivers; that is, the key buying points, or triggers, within the business that drive profitability.

An Insurance Example

Let's take a typical general insurer selling a buildings and contents (B&C) product as an example. Most people enter the market when they buy a new house for the first time. However, first-time buyers comprise a comparatively small part of the market. The NOP Financial Research Survey (FRS) indicates that only about 5 per cent of B&C buyers come from this source each year. Switchers (customers changing their insurance company allegiance) are a significantly larger sub-segment, at around 10 per cent. Both customer groups are, however, dwarfed by the average of 85 per cent who renew with the same company each year. Herein lies the difficulty. Not only do the vast proportion of customers simply renew, accepting the only quote provided by their current insurer, but nearly 55 per cent of them are (to misuse the term for the sake of convenience) 'loyal' and have been insured by the same supplier for five years or more. Customers only seek, or receive, an average of 1.6 quotations each per year. So the B&C market superficially appears inert, with minimal opportunities for growth and share gains.

The challenges become even more apparent when the reasons for seeking a quotation from a new insurer are probed. Approximately a quarter are prompted by the renewal notice; a further quarter by a personal recommendation; and one-fifth by the arrangement of a mortgage. This leaves only just over a quarter of the market to be influenced by the blandishments of any interloping marketers or sales force. So what are the key business drivers within this business? What are the things that general insurers *must* do really well if they are to be successful?

Quite obviously the renewal strategy is key, because of the degree of inertia and consumer disinterest. The happier (or perhaps less disgruntled) insurers can keep their customers, the less likely they are to shop around. The fewer quotes they seek, the less promiscuous or more inert they are likely to remain, and the lower will be the new customer-acquisition investment required in order to maintain market share. But, what is the primary determinant of a 'happy' buyer of a product that costs a lot and has few immediately apparent benefits? In the vast majority of cases, it is the very same reason that friends and family recommend different companies to each other – because of the way in which a claim was handled. So claims management and communication are also critical.

What about the acquisition of new insurance customers? In a well-managed insurer it should arguably be the lowest priority.

It is the most expensive way to maintain market share; the opportunities for growth are small; and it has the least positive leverage on business dynamics. However, where is all the effort and investment concentrated by the typical B&C insurer? You've guessed it, at the front end of the business. Expensive direct mail, costly Internet sites, the best creative talent, freephone contact – no expense is spared. Have you tried to claim recently? A local-rate telephone number (at your own expense); a multilevel menu of options; and a wait that will often be interminable before a real person deigns to speak to you.

This story illustrates the importance of rigorous analysis, not simply to be customer oriented but to be customer focused. By concentrating on the key areas of leverage and satisfaction, many companies would be able to reduce their customer acquisition budgets and improve their profitability through not only reduced costs, but also increased referrals.

The Key Points of Leverage

In most businesses, one of the key areas on which no unreasonable effort should be spared is the period immediately after the first purchase or renewal, when the maximum customer attrition occurs. No other time, barring death (or 'involuntary attrition', as it was known at one charge-card operator), has a greater influence on future purchase intentions and hence the potential value of the customers acquired. Yet it is not unusual to see far greater effort and resources directed towards the acquisition of new customers, or those that have lapsed or, indeed, those that have chosen another competitor.

A Business Parable

Whatever the business, the key is to identify the drivers of profitability and then direct the maximum effort and investment towards them – and the starting point thereafter is the specification of appropriate customer-communications objectives. This, again, might seem a statement of the blindingly obvious, but consider the following scene:

Scene: The Two Ferrets Public House
Players: Thrusting executive and bar-room pedant
Time: Thursday, 6.30 pm

Exec: My objective is to drink six pints of beer tonight.
Pedant (interrupting smugly): That's not an objective, it's a tactic.
Exec: No, it's not. I've had a lousy day and I'm going to get blitzed.
Pedant: That's not objective either, it's a strategy.
Exec: Call it what you want, I'm going to forget I ever had a day
   like today.
Pedant (triumphantly): Now that's an objective. Fancy a pint?

Hopefully, the two protagonists still felt sufficiently well disposed towards each other afterwards to be able to achieve oblivion by closing time. Apart from indicating just how boring some people can be, the conversation does help to impart a serious message to anyone involved in designing and setting objectives for managing customers, as Figure 8.2 demonstrates.

Within our, admittedly rather silly, scenario lies a serious point. Had our executive been clearer about his objective, he would have identified a variety of different strategies, apart from getting drunk. He could have visited the theatre or invited his friend for a meal, to name but two options. Had he chosen the theatrical route, he

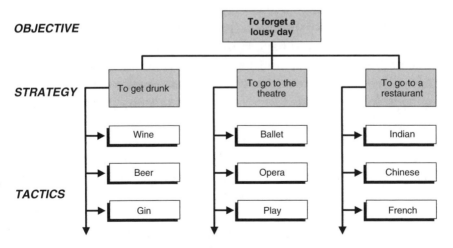

Figure 8.2 Forgetting a lousy day . . .
Reproduced with permission of Valoris Ltd

could have decided on the opera as his elected means of escapism; a very different set of tactics to the one on which he intuitively alighted!

What is an Objective?

An objective is a statement that describes, as tightly as possible, what the result of your endeavour should be. It should be measurable, so that it is possible to tell whether you have achieved it or not, and it should specify a completion date. An objective to increase profits by 10 per cent sounds laudable, but not if it takes four years when inflation is running at 3 per cent.

Consider, for example, the havoc that can be wreaked by shorthand planning that ignores this discipline. A well-known food manufacturer researched and developed a brand new range of convenience foods. The responsible manager knew from experience that the secret of sales success was point-of-sale display. Consequently, he developed a range of expensive items to support the retailer and, for good measure, sales promotion was used to encourage repeat purchase. The campaign sank without trace and our hapless product manager moved to the special projects department. Why? Because he didn't articulate his objective and plan his strategy. Had he done so, he would have identified that his objective was actually to sell a certain volume or value of product within a specified time frame and within a given cost budget. He would have known that gaining shelf space was a necessary pre-requisite and, through consideration of the tactical alternatives available to him, he might have realized that his competitors were offering the retailer advantageous purchase terms. Without the planning framework, however, he intuitively selected an inappropriate and hopelessly unsuccessful tactic.

It is an unfortunate fact of life that ill-considered objectives lead to successful customer-focused programmes by chance alone. Certainly experience plays a part, but the manager that relies solely on the past misses the opportunity to solve problems creatively and innovatively. Far from imposing rigidity, a formal, disciplined approach allows the mind to explore exciting, new alternatives within a framework that reduces clutter and improves focus.

Strategy and Tactics: What will You Actually Do?

Once the key areas of performance leverage have been defined and appropriate objectives set for each customer interaction, it is time to define the strategy and tactics. Unfortunately, there is no short cut to what can be a laborious and time-consuming activity.

Let's consider one of the country's leading furniture manufacturers by way of illustration. This company distributed its products through the retail trade and decided that it could effectively manage no more than four customer segments, which were differentiated by current customer value and distribution channel, as illustrated in Figure 8.3.

Setting the Strategy

The manufacturer therefore had high- and low-value multiple retailers and corresponding value groups among the typically smaller independent outlets. After much thought, it decided that it must introduce a key account-management programme for the high-value multiples because of the volume of business they generated. The cost of servicing the independents, on the other hand, was very high and the low-value customers within this segment did not warrant any greater investment than simply taking their orders, if and when they arose. The strategies for these two segments were clear.

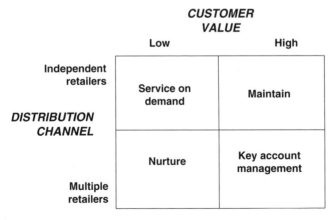

Figure 8.3   Furniture manufacture customer-segmentation model

However, the low-value multiples and high-value independents segments were far more problematic. The trend within the market was towards greater retailer consolidation and, although the company was currently securing high volumes of business from some independent retailers, it decided that its future lay with the multiples. Consequently, it set out to nurture those with low value, while simply maintaining the existing relationships that it enjoyed with the high-value independents. So segment strategies had been set that appeared to make sound business sense, but what would they actually do differently?

Developing the Tactics

With the key accounts, for example, the company established a relationship-management approach, rather than the previous model based solely on sales-force geography. It allocated the segment a dedicated marketing budget, which it used to fund joint advertising initiatives with the retailers, and it guaranteed a 90-day turnaround on all orders. These tactics demanded a change to the company's organization strategy; required improvements to its traditional marketing budgeting methods; and altered process flows within the factory so that the guarantee could be met.

For the low-value independents, on the other hand, the company established a telephone ordering service based on a smaller range of furniture that required less customization and hence complexity. The in-store servicing visits were reduced to once per annum and, rather than attempting to achieve showroom space, the company was happy to supply minimal stock and rely instead on brochure-based sales.

The planning and implementation phases took well over a year to complete. Some retailers were mightily upset, others were delighted. Within two years, sales had increased by 35 per cent while profits had risen by 22 per cent. In this particular case, the strategy was well founded on meaningful, value-based segments, and the tactics directed time and money towards those customers with the greatest long-term potential.

The Appraisal Process

Achieving success such as this demanded rigorous appraisal of all the different ideas that surfaced during the planning phase. A variety of different methodologies were applied, although all related to the realization of greater customer focus. The investment required was assessed against the ease of implementation. The expected increase in revenues was calculated and contrasted with the risk of failure, should the low-investment segment customers withdraw their business. And the cost of the whole reorganization was contrasted with the perceived degree of competitive differentiation that the company believed it would achieve. The company was, therefore, as reasonably sure as it could ever be that its chosen strategies, and the tactics that lay behind them, would result in profitable business growth.

The appraisal process is critical. It demands the development of financial models and significant customer understanding borne from analysis and experience. It is time consuming and often frustrating as seemingly 'good ideas' are consigned to the wastebasket. However, the results are usually more than worth the effort.

CHANNEL STRATEGIES AND IMPLEMENTATION

Unfortunately, the planning process is still incomplete. In many cases, there will still be a need to decide which distribution channels should be used and how they should be managed. For the furniture manufacturer, the various channels used were an integral part of its chosen strategies; for others, the situation is often a great deal less clear.

Channel Characteristics

Imagine a company with multiple customer communications channels such as face-to-face retail, the telephone, the Internet, above-the-line advertising and direct mail. All have their own characteristics, strengths and weaknesses. Face-to-face is often the most successful sales channel, but it is also by far and away the most expensive. The Internet is typically very cheap, but it is also very passive. The cost per customer contact for above-the-line advertising is very low, while direct mail is many times more expensive but can be far more cost-effective – if targeted well.

Reinforcing the Business Model

Each channel must be appraised for its ability to achieve the specified sales and cost objectives while, simultaneously, reinforcing the company's business model, market positioning and aspirations.

A direct bank, by definition, has no branches; but would above-the-line advertising be better than direct mail or direct-response press advertising? This was just the dilemma that faced First Direct when it launched. In retrospect, the issue appears easy and was solved by asking two, very simple questions. Is it possible to launch a new bank credibly without above-the-line advertising? No. Is it possible to acquire a sufficient volume of new customers without highly effective below-the-line support? No. Both had to work effectively together to achieve the success that the company has subsequently enjoyed.

In many instances, the answer may not appear as clear cut and will be dependent on the value of the customer and the chosen method of segmentation. Often, less confident, less experienced and frequently low-value customers seek the reassurance provided by face-to-face contact. Those that are more sophisticated, and higher value, are frequently more at ease doing their own research and buying remotely – and herein lies the rub. The most attractive customers, in terms of both costs and revenues, are in most cases the most difficult to reach and influence.

There are no easy answers and we have no panacea. The key is an in-depth understanding of customer value and needs; a very clear appreciation of competitors; and a business model that allows such trade-off calculations to be made with a degree of certainty. It isn't easy and there is very little science, which is why testing is so critical.

TESTING AND PERFORMANCE MEASUREMENT

'Quite frankly, not everyone who applies for an American Express Card is accepted.' So began a test direct-mail letter aimed at prospects for the American Express green card. The letter was being tested against the previously most successful missive, and was based on the hypothesis that its blatant snob appeal would be irresistible to many at the time. Nobody could have foreseen the results. The copy obviously caught the mood of the moment and response levels went through the roof. Hundreds of tests, over many years, were conducted in an attempt to beat this 'snob control'. Eventually one did and the company's card-member acquisition programme continued its success.

Know your Audience

Some years later, a trade magazine published a critique of a GUS direct-mail package by the managing director of a London-based advertising agency that damned its creative standards. The marketing director at the mail-order giant was understandably angry and challenged the author's company to produce something better. GUS would pay all costs and establish valid testing, but reserved the right to publish the results. The challenge was taken up and the work duly commenced. Unfortunately, the ad agency boss was unaware that the direct-mail package he had so roundly slated was enjoying outstanding results. Although it was undoubtedly unappealing to this southern-based, educated, affluent male, it pulled a train among C2D female mail-order agents. The test for the new package sank without trace, with customers responding at levels of approximately one-fifth of the established control. GUS was gracious enough never to embarrass the gentleman concerned in print.

Testing as Part of Corporate Culture

Testing should be an essential part of any company's customer-focus programme, for a number of reasons. It is impossible to be right all the time. However skilled and experienced you are, customers will always surprise you. Testing therefore reduces risk and maintains continuous learning and momentum. It allows new ideas and emerging hypotheses to be validated in the market, helping the company to strive for improved commercial performance.

Drayton Bird, a guru of direct marketing, once said that testing provides the 'opportunity to know, rather than guess'. Yet how many companies test new initiatives before they roll them out? Within established direct-marketing companies the disciple is rigorously followed; elsewhere, testing has become a forgotten art. How many businesses test the relative return in investment that will be achieved from a change of communications media, the introduction of a new medium, a new creative approach or a new pricing strategy? How many companies pilot their customer-focus initiatives in a small and controlled test prior to spending vast sums on new technological 'solutions'?

When asked by his board what the return would be on a multi-million-pound investment in new customer-management software, one director of a high-street bank simply made up the figure. Unfortunately, the board held him accountable for the target and he now works elsewhere, outside the banking industry.

Setting Control Groups

The success of the Switch debit card is, in no small way, attributable to testing. The scheme had the foresight to maintain control regions within which no advertising was ever placed. In this way, scheme management was able to quantify the impact of its cardholder communications and, by doing so, proved to its shareholders (who also comprised its Board) the importance of their continued investment in card-usage growth.

In another example, a major energy supplier saved itself a fortune by hot-housing a new idea prior to investing in new technology. It created a small team with telephones, stand-alone PCs and can-do attitudes – and told the team members to prove the case. They did, and the practical experience enabled them to develop a far clearer technology specification that was implemented more quickly, and with greater certainty, than would have been the case otherwise.

The Strengths of Testing

Testing has various strengths, if designed well and implemented professionally. It measures actual customer performance, whether it is an initial purchase, a cross-sale, an up-sale, a renewal rate or whatever. The results should be statistically significant, so that the probability of repetition is known prior to implementation. Testing allows complete customer propositions (or each of the discrete variables within the proposition) to be validated, such that managers know whether product A, through channel B, aimed at customer group C, at price D, in month E will produce an acceptable return. And it can be conducted discreetly, so that new initiatives often pass beneath competitors' radar until they are proven, providing the testing organization with significant commercial advantage.

Critics of testing will use a variety of arguments. They will say that it measures what people buy, but not why. They will say that it tells you what has happened, not what will happen. They will say that it is expensive, in both actual and opportunity cost. And they will say that it takes too long, potentially losing competitive initiative. All are possibly true, but none is insurmountable with the judicious addition of a little customer research and a lot of commercial common sense.

A Little Knowledge?

A little knowledge may be said to be a dangerous thing – but ignorance is expensive. Testing should be an integral part of every company's customer-focus strategy. Customers learn, their behaviour changes and markets mature. Competitors are continuously evolving and new market entrants appear. New technologies are changing the way people think, act and interact. The economic and social environments are continually changing. All these factors demand that companies must consistently challenge the status quo and look for new, and more profitable, ways of doing business. Testing can often provide the answers.

CUSTOMER AND MARKET KNOWLEDGE MANAGEMENT

More complete nonsense is talked about customer and market knowledge management than practically any other aspect of customer focus. Unsurprisingly, there is a very persuasive group of IT sales people who would have you believe that knowledge-management technology provides the only solution. Rubbish. To borrow a phrase from scuba diving, many companies 'have all the gear and no idea'.

The Basic Questions

Technology allows you to store, sort, analyse and retrieve, and it can often perform all these tasks very quickly. As such, it can provide a very useful service for companies that have a clear idea about what it is they need to collect, store, sort, analyse and retrieve in the first place. For others that are struggling to gain a better understanding of their customers and markets, it can be an expensive distraction. Before incurring even more investment, ask yourself some basic questions.

Does your organization have a fully up-to-date and constantly maintained library of all relevant market research studies, comprising both bought-in and specially commissioned research; or is this only available to the commissioning manager and his or her team, who use the knowledge as a weapon for fighting internal battles? Does your company routinely collect and analyse competitor information and intelligence, relating to all aspects of the competitors' businesses; or are such analyses performed (if at all) by many different people who study only those competitor activities that are relevant to them? Does your company regularly analyse market dynamics and assess the strategic implications of the evolving marketplace? If the answer to any of these questions is negative, it is unlikely that technology will be of any great assistance: your knowledge-management issues are rather more deep-seated.

Knowledge should be a Corporate Asset

For most companies, including many FTSE 100 quoted firms, the questions posed above would be challenging. Information and intelligence are frequently collected and analysed on an *ad hoc* basis, often in response to a specific request by senior management. They are also compartmentalized or, perhaps more accurately, departmentalized, in as much as they remain within the confines of the commissioning department. And, perhaps most damning of all, they are simply lost or thrown away. How often do companies make the same mistakes, year in and year out, because intelligence and knowledge are lost through staff turnover? Rather than becoming a corporate asset, it becomes instead a personal asset, aggrandizing the manager not the owner.

If your company is struggling with knowledge management, start simply. Build an intranet; make sure that it is regularly updated with all *relevant* results, research, information and intelligence; encourage staff to contribute to it; and make it a hanging offence for it to be incomplete or out of date. Invest in more sophisticated technology only when you are routinely collecting, analysing and acting on the information gathered. Any other route is likely to end in very expensive tears.

CHANGE PLANNING

It is outside the scope of this book to provide a step-by-step guide to change management. We simply recognize it as a vital ingredient that must not be overlooked. Any customer-focus programme will have an impact on people's jobs, the ways they think and the things they do. It requires thoughtful and expert planning to ensure an orderly and successful transition. Do not underestimate the scope of the task. Some people will be advocates of change; some will be indifferent; some will be openly resistant. All will move at different speeds and require careful management.

The Challenge of the New

Introducing more customer-focused strategies and plans will also require new internal processes to be developed and perhaps existing ones refined in order to recognize the changes and reap the commercial benefits. New customer- and knowledge-management strategies may require new technological support; and new customer-segmentation models will require new ways of working and, perhaps, a new organization structure. Operations will change and the processes designed to realize the advantages must change also. All must be documented. The extent of retraining and personnel planning may also be considerable: to transfer new skills, to change job descriptions and previous practices, and to introduce and cement new ways of thinking and behaving.

Plan for Change

It may be that the skills to manage such change exist within the organization. More likely, expert external assistance will have to be sought. Seek advice as early as practical in the programme, so that the scope and nature of the change issues can be identified and the necessary programme planned. It is unrealistic to believe that change will occur 'naturally' once the strategies and plans are all in place. Senior management may be convinced of the need to do things differently, but it may take rather longer to win the hearts and minds of others who are not as close to the strategic rationale.

TECHNOLOGY STRATEGY

Finally, a few words on technology. The casual reader of this book might come to the conclusion that we are not great fans. In fact, nothing could be further from the truth. In our own company, we invested in personal computers when golf-ball typewriters were still the norm. We networked our systems as soon as it became possible to do so. We used internal e-mail before it was possible to send messages externally. We built our own intranet and managed our knowledge though a shared access area. Over the years, we worked with many clients at the cutting edge of the application of new technologies. Indeed, so convinced were we that technology was changing the future and the art of the possible, we actively sought a technology partnership for our business – and ultimately sold our company to the technology consultancy that we selected.

We are unashamedly discussing technology last not to denigrate its importance or the impact that it can have, but simply because this book has been about developing greater customer focus and the mindless application of the latest technology has frequently done more harm than good. Many great companies have believed the slick words of the technology sales forces and bought (or, perhaps, been sold) 'solutions' that have reduced customer focus and alienated the very customers that they sought to serve.

The Changing Role of IT

Some years ago, the IT role was clear. The strategists decided what the company would or should do and the technologists made it all happen, as far as they were able. It was neat and everyone knew where they were. Everything has changed. New media, hardware and software, with outstanding capabilities, have been developed (and are constantly being introduced) providing functionalities that were only dreamed of previously and that frequently surpass even the optimistic seer's wildest expectations. Technology is now a key facet of many companies' competitive strategy. No longer do the technologists simply follow, they also have a leadership role: identifying new business models; new ways to distribute products and services; new ways of interacting with customers; new ways of identifying profitable (and unprofitable) customers and managing the relationships accordingly.

It is therefore essential that technologists play a pivotal role in the development of greater customer focus; they are essential members of the team. Technology can assist with customer segmentation and the implementation of a profitable customer-management strategy. It can help manage the customer and market knowledge within a business. It can assist with testing and will have a vital role to play in performance measurement and reporting. It will frequently have an impact on processes and the way in which customer-facing managers interact with customers.

However, customer focus is about identifying an appropriate competitive strategy, understanding customer needs and values, and satisfying those needs and realizing the potential value, as far as it is profitable to do so. New technologies can help facilitate the realization of customer focus and can sometimes lead to quantum steps in competitive strategy, but rarely should technologists lead the charge and there are few questions about customer focus for which technology is the only answer. In far too many cases, technology has been bought as a substitute for thought, a panacea. The role of technology remains to deliver a company's chosen strategy more effectively, or efficiently. It must not replace nor substitute for the basic principles outlined in this book.

Key Principles

Rant over. What are the key issues to consider when setting your technology strategy and its role in your customer-focus programme?

- Ensure that technologists are involved at all stages of your customer-focus programme from the outset. They can often offer insights, solutions and new opportunities that are simply unknown and invisible to others without experience and knowledge.
- Allow technologists to adopt a leadership role only when the technology itself is the primary element of your chosen, and appraised, business strategy – or when you have an exceptional IT director.
- Never believe that technology offers a panacea. New business models such as those employed by many of the newer direct-to-consumer companies, or those based on Internet distribution, have been developed. However, most had the benefit of starting with a clean sheet of paper and, even so, many of these technology-led business models have been fundamentally flawed in terms of their customer propositions. For the majority of companies, the role of technology still remains to support and, as such, it must not substitute for rational business analysis and acumen.
- Always construct a business case and question the assumptions used within it. If, for example, greater sales or customer longevity are forecast, ask to see the test results, contact the client companies given as sales case studies and question the logic of the assumptions against your own business experience.
- Never brief consultants to integrate a packaged technology solution before the development of your customer-focus strategy. It will be far more expensive than you imagine; it will take longer to implement than is forecast; and the consultants are unlikely to be able to provide you with the necessary insight into what you should actually do with it when you have it.

- Always compare technology suppliers against a pre-determined list of functionalities and deliverables. Do not become seduced by the art of the possible, seek to meet articulated business needs only. If the potential suppliers surprise you with new ideas and uses that you have not considered, fire the technologists that have been advising you on the programme and rethink your strategy!

A final note of reassurance: if the advice given in this book seems daunting or beyond the capabilities of your organization, take heart from the fact that the majority of your competitors feel exactly the same way. One of the most common questions asked of us was to identify which companies could be regarded as role models. The answer was always the same – none. To our knowledge, not one company in the UK has introduced *all* of the ideas and thoughts detailed in these pages. Some have been very successful with value-based customer management; some with enhanced segmentation; some with the introduction of new ways of thinking; some with new technological support. Does this render the search for improvement unworthy? You decide.

Index

AA, 13, 149
accounting, 82, 85, 92, 93, 95, 107
added value, 56, 114, 115, 133
Air Miles, 114, 159, 160
Alliance & Leicester, 159
Amazon, 66, 149
American Express, 59, 208, 209
Asda, 158
averaging, 87
Axa, 59

Bang & Olufsen, 66
Barclaycard, 10, 60, 158
benchmarking, 44, 45, 46, 171
benefits, 11, 12, 17, 20, 23, 26, 28, 67,
    75, 92, 109, 115, 143, 146–160, 163,
    182, 185, 201, 213
best-in-class, 44, 46, 170
BMW, 159
BP, 13
brand, 5, 16, 18, 20, 51, 52, 54, 59, 66,
    77, 83, 84, 101, 115, 148–151, 158,
    171, 197, 204
branding, 151, 184
British Airways, 13, 200

British Rail, 66
budget, 6, 95, 191, 204, 206
budgeting, 23, 206
budgets, 110, 152, 202
business strategy, 37, 49, 200, 216
business-to-business, 13, 36–37, 56,
    117, 152, 186, 198

call centre, 3, 154, 167, 169, 172–173,
    178
change, 10, 16, 17, 22, 29, 31, 49, 57,
    62, 69, 95, 125, 135, 138, 141–143,
    154–158, 164, 167–170, 176–183,
    187, 191, 192, 206, 210, 213, 214
commitment, 31, 54, 81, 108, 138, 142,
    149, 170, 180, 192
competitive advantage, 4, 18, 19, 53,
    67, 109, 129, 137, 144, 147, 178
competitive strategy, 61, 62, 65, 77, 96,
    115, 117, 138, 195, 215
corporate strategy, 27, 65
cost control, 55, 95
cost leadership, 70, 72
costs, 5–8, 10, 11, 21, 24, 26, 32, 56, 57,
    60, 63, 76, 79, 80, 84, 85, 91, 93,

95–99, 103, 104, 108, 112, 113, 119, 132, 134, 137, 150–152, 157, 162, 163, 174, 177, 178, 188, 191, 192, 198–202, 208, 209
Coutts, 59
creativity, 46, 54, 63, 144, 192
CRM, 5, 18, 26, 27, 176, 189
cross-sales, 5, 10, 19, 26, 66, 99–100, 107, 120, 123, 196, 199
current value, 100, 102, 103, 105
customer acquisition, 8, 9, 11, 56, 63, 76, 84, 99, 103, 110, 117, 150, 155, 198, 199, 202
customer attitudes, 39, 151, 160
customer attrition, 14, 102, 202
customer behaviour, 5, 13, 16, 18, 21, 22, 42, 75, 115, 130, 133, 136, 138, 170–171, 176
customer characteristics, 25
customer communications, 127, 172, 191, 194, 207
customer correspondence, 48, 157
customer data, 23, 25–26, 77, 120, 136, 162, 176
customer database, 120, 136, 176
customer defection, 8, 13, 87, 125
customer dynamics, 77
customer expectations, 162
customer focus, 3, 4, 18, 21, 25–31, 35, 46, 53, 57, 68, 76, 80, 85, 97, 109, 113, 121, 138–145, 149, 150, 154, 157, 159, 162, 164, 166, 169–171, 176, 177, 179, 180, 183, 185–202, 207, 211, 214, 215
customer insight, 46, 96, 109
customer investment, 27, 102, 155, 199
customer leadership, 1, 2, 4
customer led, 1, 2, 3, 4
customer lifecycle, 73, 76
customer lifetime, 16, 75, 98–102, 105, 107, 108, 110, 117, 121, 125, 150
customer longevity, 88, 122, 123, 130, 216

customer motivations, 71
customer needs, 2, 52, 54, 77–80, 98, 117, 145, 154, 178, 215
customer orientation, 57, 74, 187
customer ownership, 185
customer performance, 22, 26, 82, 91, 96–97, 113, 120, 124, 129, 134, 210
customer perspective, 31, 58
customer profitability, 18, 40, 54, 71, 76, 91, 113, 132, 142–143, 148, 171, 194, 198
customer referral, 93, 104
customer relationship management, 5, 18, 21
customer relationships, 18, 19, 21, 40, 159, 186
customer retention, 15, 19, 88, 107, 125
customer satisfaction, 2, 4, 5, 12, 14, 15, 57, 172
customer segments, 57, 60, 61, 70, 76, 94, 107, 112, 128, 194, 198, 205
customer service, 27, 66, 68, 87, 91, 95, 103, 108, 135, 141, 154, 156, 163, 167, 175
customer sophistication, 115
customer strategy, 21, 51, 65, 82
customer understanding, 21, 31, 46, 47, 115, 118, 196, 207
customer value, 9, 18, 20, 25, 32, 46, 49, 70, 71, 76, 91, 93, 97–104, 108, 110, 113, 119, 127, 133, 136, 155, 159, 194, 205, 208

data, 21, 23, 26, 35, 39–41, 46, 61, 87–89, 94, 96, 97, 108, 120, 121, 136–138, 145, 162, 176, 177, 195, 197
analysis, 41, 88, 120, 136, 197
collection, 121
management, 137
Dell, 66
differentiation, 18, 27, 56, 63, 66, 67, 68, 71, 72, 105, 109, 144, 207

Direct Line, 13, 72
distribution, 7, 16, 22, 31, 55, 60, 84,
    86, 87, 91, 117, 124, 128, 137, 150,
    151, 186, 187, 192, 205, 207, 216
Drayton Bird, 209
due diligence, 83, 84, 97

Egg, 57, 151
Enron, 157
Esso, 13

features, 20, 66, 68, 69, 101, 146–147,
    159, 173
finance, 92, 127, 142–143, 165
First Direct, 57, 68, 151, 158, 208
fixed costs, 12, 99, 152
focus groups, 34

Girobank, 159
Go, 200
Guinness, 66
GUS, 209

HSBC, 57

Igor Ansoff, 64–65
incentives, 17, 84, 89, 114–115, 148,
    158, 174–175, 198
indirect costs, 12
inducements, 17, 18, 76
innovation, 54, 68, 109, 133, 182, 192
IT, 26–28, 43, 147, 188, 191, 211,
    215–216

key account management, 38
Kuoni, 68

Lastminute.com, 149
listening, 2, 32–39, 43, 46, 47
Lloyds TSB, 3, 158
Lunn Poly, 13

management information, 46, 86, 93,
    102

management information systems, 93
Marconi, 157
marketing, 5–7, 21–27, 35, 40, 48, 56,
    86, 91, 98–99, 101, 109, 115, 117,
    119–120, 127, 141, 153, 163, 165,
    166, 176, 191, 206, 209, 210
Marks & Spencer, 34, 200
MBNA, 32
measurement, 85, 88, 92, 194, 196, 208,
    215
MI, 93–95
Michael Porter, 61–62, 66
Microsoft, 2, 3
Midland Bank, 60, 66, 151
Mike Harris, 151
MIS, 93, 96–97, 107, 173
mystery shopping, 49

NatWest, 60
new product development, 143,
    145–146

objectives, 9, 24, 25, 28, 52–55, 58, 59,
    74, 77, 79, 82, 99, 100, 107,
    129–137, 156, 161, 172, 174, 177,
    187, 189, 193, 197–205, 208
one-to-one marketing, 21–25
overheads, 7, 11, 57, 70, 84, 95, 99, 103,
    135

potential value, 25, 31, 41, 54, 94,
    97–108, 114, 126, 127, 195, 198,
    202, 215
processes, 6, 31, 43, 45, 145, 177, 189,
    191, 192, 194–195, 213, 215
product strategy, 143
profit hierarchy, 64–65
proposition, 7, 15, 18, 31, 40, 52, 69, 70,
    71, 74–76, 86, 87, 94, 112, 114, 115,
    128, 134, 146–151, 176, 198, 200,
    211
Prudential, 151

quick wins, 78, 196

repeat purchase, 17, 70, 123, 148, 159, 160, 204

research, 30, 32, 35, 38–41, 45, 46, 48, 80, 86, 129, 131, 134, 161, 197, 208, 211–213

Richer Sounds, 68

Royal Bank of Scotland, 60

Sainsbury, 158

sales, 2, 7, 17–27, 34–37, 45, 64, 69, 71, 73, 75, 79, 81, 96, 99, 112, 113, 117, 120, 127, 129, 132, 133, 141, 148, 163–166, 174–176, 186, 191, 193, 195, 198, 201, 204–208, 211, 214, 216

SBU, 184

segmentation, 25, 41, 92, 107–139, 196, 205, 208, 213, 215, 217

shareholder value, 21, 31, 33, 36, 44, 45, 49, 53, 79, 85, 127, 157, 198, 199

Sony, 2–3

strategic business unit, 184

strategy, 2, 9, 11, 19–21, 38, 49–59, 63, 64, 66, 69, 70, 72, 77–85, 91, 92, 102, 108–115, 124, 130–138, 144, 149, 152, 158, 161, 162, 174, 175, 177, 178, 182, 188, 192, 194, 195, 200–217

Swatch, 68

tactics, 53, 55, 81, 82, 200, 204–207

targeting, 18, 128

technological, 5, 21, 62, 151, 189, 191, 210, 213, 217

technologies, 5, 6, 19, 25–31, 56, 63, 176, 192, 195, 211, 214, 215

technology, 23, 38, 42, 43, 55, 72, 142, 150, 152, 167, 175–177, 189, 191, 192, 210–217

Tesco, 158, 160

test, 13, 18, 22, 126, 134, 135, 147, 153, 155, 208–210, 216

testing, 25, 112, 124, 134, 135, 191, 194, 208–215

Thomas Cook, 13

TQM, 168

tracking, 38, 86, 178

Trailfinders, 70

up-sales, 100, 107, 120, 123, 199

variable costs, 65, 91

vision, 3, 4, 22, 28, 52–54, 58, 59, 133, 180, 187, 193

Waitrose, 158

WorldCom, 157